Selling You!

Selling You!

NAPOLEON HILL

Selling You! is the most complete compilation of material
created and written by Napoleon Hill on the subjects of selling,
salesmanship, marketing your personal services, and selling yourself.

Edited by Bill Hartley

Contributing editor: Ann Hartley

HIGHROADS
MEDIA, INC.

ISBN-10: 1-932429-26-3
ISBN-13: 978-1-932429-26-8

10 9 8 7 6 5 4 3 2

CONTENTS

Chapter I

EVERYONE IS SELLING

Thirty-five years ago a young man dropped from a moving freight train in West Orange, New Jersey, and hurriedly made his way to the laboratory of Thomas A. Edison. When asked to state his business, before being permitted to see Mr. Edison, the young man boldly replied, "I am going to become his partner!"

His boldness got him past the secretary. An hour later he was at work, scrubbing floors in the Edison plant. That hour of selling was worth millions of dollars. The young man was Edwin C. Barnes. Five years later he was a partner of the great Edison, and he became famous as the distributor of Edison's dictating machine that revolutionized the way businesses operated.

Edwin Barnes accumulated a fortune and he owed every cent of it to the hour he spent in private conversation with Edison. During that hour he sold himself so thoroughly that it gave him his opportunity to go into partnership with one of the greatest men this country ever produced.

My own first job was that of secretary to General Rufus A. Ayers. I started working for him while I was still in my teens, and before I was twenty I became the general manager of one of Rufus Ayers' coal mines. The jump from secretary to general manager was made in less than one hour, during which I sold myself to him by voluntarily doing a service for which I neither expected nor asked for pay. That sale changed my life and led directly to my alliance with Andrew Carnegie, which has ultimately affected millions of people around the world.

At the request of Andrew Carnegie, I began to research all causes of success and failure, and to organize the results into a philosophy of individual achievement. The facts described in this book were not merely written; they were lived by the men and women who made America the greatest industrial nation on earth. I got the facts directly from those people. For thirty years I had the collaboration of America's most creative and successful entrepreneurs, inventors, businessmen, industrialists, and political leaders.

During all those years of research I interviewed and gained the cooperation of more than 500 of the most successful men and women in the world, including Henry Ford, Thomas A. Edison, Luther Burbank, President Woodrow Wilson, John D. Rockefeller, Harvey S. Firestone, William Wrigley Jr., F. W. Woolworth, and scores of others who sold themselves into fabulous riches—with the aid of the same principles of selling you will find in this book.

EDITOR'S NOTE

Few people have ever understood salesmanship as well as Napoleon Hill. In addition to being world-famous as the author of the bestselling self-help books of all time, Hill became a legend in business circles for personally teaching salesmanship so effectively that he turned around failing companies by multiplying sales many times over. He not only taught salespeople how to double and triple their income, but he also created college-level courses on advertising and sales, then sold the colleges on the concept of making his courses part of their curriculum.

Although Hill's philosophy of personal achievement was rooted in the secrets of success told to him by the leaders of business and industry, he also learned some of the lessons the hard way, having personally launched a number of startup companies that made fortunes then lost everything, some due to war, others to the Depression. He sold ideas to some of America's biggest companies, he settled major labor disputes by selling both management and labor on new and better ways to work together, and he helped two presidents to sell America to Americans during hard times when the average man on the street was losing faith in the future.

W. Clement Stone, who was himself renowned for his ability to turn cold calls into sales, was so impressed with Hill's ability that Stone asked Hill to take charge of creating a new sales program for his insurance company, Combined Insurance Company (now known as Aon Corporation). As you will read in the chapter on Master Mind alliances, Combined Insurance was already big, but the sales course Hill created turned it into a giant.

Selling You! *offers the most complete exploration of Napoleon Hill's approach to sales and selling yourself. In preparing this edition, the editors conducted an extensive review of Hill's books, speeches, lectures, articles, and recordings to find the best explanations, examples, anecdotes, and illustrations. The structure of the book is based upon the sales-oriented chapters from Napoleon Hill's* How to Sell Your Way Through Life, *augmented by the relevant chapters and excerpts from Hill's four-volume masterwork,* Law of Success, *and his classic bestseller,* Think and Grow Rich: The 21st-Century Edition. *This edition also features examples and anecdotes from Hill's other works, including selections from* Believe and Achieve *and from* Napoleon Hill's Keys to Success, *as well as material from* The Success System That Never Fails *by W. Clement Stone, and* A Lifetime of Riches: The Biography of Napoleon Hill *by Michael J. Ritt Jr. and Kirk Landers.*

In preparing this new and updated edition, where material might be considered dated or out of step with contemporary practices, the original text has been updated or augmented with relevant new material.

In addition to contemporary examples, where the editors felt it would be of interest to the reader, we have included notes that provide relevant information about more recent developments. We have also suggested books and other materials that complement various aspects of Napoleon Hill's philosophy.

Further, the editors have approached the written text as we would that of a living author. When we encountered what modern grammarians would consider to be run-on sentences, outdated punctuation, or other matters of form, we opted for contemporary usage.

As noted previously, the basic structure of Selling You! *is based on an adaptation of the text from* How to Sell Your Way Through Life. *In many cases the basic text has been adapted or elaborated upon by carefully integrating into it other material originally published in* Law of Success *or* Think and Grow Rich: The 21st-Century Edition. *In those instances where the editors have inserted complete paragraphs or longer segments from these two publications or from Hill's other writings, the additional material and the original source are clearly identified. All editorial commentary and new examples are clearly set off in a font and style that is different from Napoleon Hill's text.*

EVERYONE IS SELLING ALL THE TIME

The ability to influence people without irritating them is the most profitable skill you can learn. This book is devoted to teaching you the principles of psychology through which you can negotiate with others without friction. These principles were learned from the life experiences of some of the most successful leaders in business, industry, finance, and education.

Life is a series of ever-changing and shifting circumstances. No two experiences are exactly alike. No two people are exactly alike. This makes it necessary for us to adapt ourselves to others who think and act differently than we do. Our success depends on how well we negotiate our way through these daily contacts with other people without friction or opposition.

Salesmanship, as the term is used in this book, applies not only to marketing goods and services but it also applies to selling you and your personality. As a matter of fact, the major object in writing this book is to teach you how to sell yourself by using the same strategies and psychology that master salespeople use in selling goods and services.

Everyone is selling all the time. No matter who you are, every time you meet someone, explain an idea, talk on the telephone, or give an opinion, you are selling your most valuable asset: you. If you are looking for work, you have to sell yourself to be hired, and then you must continue to sell yourself to keep your job. If you go to the bank for a loan, you must sell the banker on making the loan. Teachers sell lessons. Politicians sell themselves into office. Ministers sell their sermons. And lawyers sell their clients' cases to the judges and juries.

Any form of effort through which one person persuades another to cooperate is salesmanship. Most efforts to sell are weak, and for this reason most people are poor salespeople.

Schooling, college degrees, or intellect will not do you much good if you can't get other people to cooperate with you in order to create opportunities for yourself. Those qualities may help you make the most of an opportunity once you get it, but first you must create the opportunity to be worked on. You must create opportunity by selling your goods, your services, your ideas, your ability, your personality, yourself.

The whole of any life can be seen as one long, unbroken chain of sales. Following are five very formal definitions of salesmanship, written by Jean Beltrand:

1. Selling is the ability to make known your faith, goods, or propositions to a person or persons to a point of creating a desire for a privilege, an opportunity, a possession, or an interest.

2. Selling is the ability of professional and public persons to render services, assistance, and cooperation to a point of creating a desire on the part of the people to remunerate, recognize, and honor.

3. Selling is the ability to perform work, duties, and services as an employee, to a point of creating a desire on the part of an employer to remunerate, promote, and praise.

4. Selling is the ability to be polite, kind, agreeable, and considerate to a point of creating a desire upon the part of those you meet to respect, love, and honor you.

5. Selling is the ability to write, design, paint, invent, create, compose, or accomplish anything to a point of creating a desire upon the part of others to acclaim its possessors as heroes, celebrities, and persons of greatness.

I would add to that list my own favorite definition: Selling is the art of planting in the mind of another a motive that will induce favorable action.

We are all salespeople, regardless of what our job is. But not all of us are master salespeople.

- The master salesperson becomes a master because of his or her ability to induce other people to act upon motives without resistance or friction.

- Master salespeople know what they want. They know how to plan the acquiring of what they want. Moreover, they have the initiative to put their plan into action.

- The master salesperson's education is not complete unless he or she has the ability to persuade or influence groups of people, not just individuals. The ability to speak to groups with force and conviction is a priceless asset. But it must be learned. It is an art that can be acquired only through study, effort, and experience.

- A master salesperson has the ability to influence people through the printed page as well as by the spoken word.

- A master salesperson is an artist who can paint word-pictures as skillfully as Rembrandt could blend colors on a canvas.

- A master salesperson is a strategist at mind manipulation.

- A master salesperson is a philosopher who can interpret causes by their effects and effects by their causes.

- A master salesperson is a character analyst.

- A master salesperson knows what thoughts are in people's minds by the expressions on their faces, by the words they speak, by their silence, and by the "feeling" you get from within while you are in their presence.

- A master salesperson can predict the future by observing what has happened in the past.

- A master salesperson is the master of others because he or she masters himself or herself.

No matter who you are or how much you know, you will not succeed unless you are a salesperson. You must sell your services. You must sell your knowledge. You must sell your personality. You must sell yourself.

If you master these fundamental principles of persuasion you can sell your way through life successfully, surmounting obstacles, overcoming opposition, harnessing and redirecting adverse forces.

QUALITIES A MASTER SALESPERSON MUST HAVE

Following is a list of 28 qualities that any salesperson must work to develop. The first five qualities are absolutely necessary if you want to be a master salesperson:

1. *Courage* must be part of every person who succeeds in any undertaking, especially that of selling in times of intense competition.

2. *Imagination* is an absolute necessity. You must anticipate situations and objections from prospective customers, and you must have the imagination to put yourself into your customer's position so you can understand their needs and objectives. You must almost literally stand in the other person's shoes. This takes real imagination.

3. *The way you speak* and your tone of voice must be pleasing. A meek or uncertain voice indicates a weak person. A firm, clear voice that moves with assurance and color indicates a person with enthusiasm and aggressiveness.

4. *Physical fitness* is of utmost importance for the simple reason that neither mind nor body can function well without it. You must give attention to proper diet, healthful exercise, and fresh air.

5. *Hard work* is the only thing that will turn sales training and ability into money. No amount of good health, courage, or imagination is worth a dime unless it is put to work, and the amount you make is usually fixed by the amount of very hard, intelligent work that you actually put out.

The above-listed principles are simple. There is nothing unusual or even striking in them. But most salespeople fail to possess one or more of these five primary requisites. Some salespeople may work hard and use their imaginations well, until they meet a succession of turndowns. It is here that the salesperson with courage comes right back and whips the salesperson who doesn't have these qualities. Courage is essential.

Then again, many salespeople exhibit courage, imagination, and hard work, but through laziness, drugs, or alcohol they don't have the physical stamina to stick to it when the going gets tough. Following are eight more essential qualities. These pertain to the product or service being sold, and to the sales plan and strategy:

6. *Knowledge of the merchandise.* The master salesperson analyzes carefully the merchandise or service, and understands thoroughly its every advantage. The master salesperson knows that if you do not understand and believe in the product or service, you cannot successfully sell it.

7. *Belief in the merchandise or service.* The master salesperson never tries to sell anything in which he or she does not have confidence. Master salespeople know that regardless of what they may say about their

wares, their minds will broadcast their lack of confidence to the mind of the prospective buyer.

8. *Appropriateness of merchandise.* The master salesperson analyzes both the prospective buyer and the buyer's needs, and offers only that which is appropriate to both. The master salesperson never tries to sell a Rolls-Royce to a person who ought to purchase a Ford. A bad bargain for the buyer is a worse bargain for the seller.

9. *Value given.* The master salesperson never tries to get more than the products are actually worth. The confidence and goodwill of the prospective buyer is worth more than the profit on a single sale.

10. *Knowledge of the prospective buyer.* The true master salesperson must be a character analyst. A master at selling has the ability to ascertain which of the nine basic motives the buyer will respond to most freely. The real salesperson builds the sales presentation around those motives.

11. *Qualifying the prospective buyer.* The master salesperson never tries to make a sale until he or she has properly "qualified" the prospective buyer. The master salesperson has calculated in advance the following points:

    • The prospective buyer's financial capacity to purchase.

    • The prospective buyer's need for what is being offered for sale.

    • The prospective buyer's motive in making the purchase.

    Trying to make sales without first qualifying the prospective buyer is a mistake that stands at the head of the list of causes of "no sale."

12. *Ability to "neutralize" the mind of the buyer.* The master salesperson knows that no sale can be made until the mind of the prospective buyer has been neutralized, or made receptive. The master salesperson will not endeavor to close a sale until he or she has opened the mind of the buyer and prepared it as a background or base upon which to put together the word-mosaic of the sales pitch.

13. *Ability to close a sale.* Supersales stars are artists at reaching the closing point in selling and they train themselves to sense the right psychological moment. They rarely if ever ask the prospective buyer if he or she is ready to purchase. Instead, the real masters simply assume that the buyer is ready to buy. Here they use the power of suggestion most effectively. The supersales stars avoid trying to close a sale until they know in their own mind that they can close successfully. They conduct their sales presentations so that the prospect believes he or she has done the buying.

Following are the final 15 principles to be acquired. These have more to do with the personal makeup and self-organization of the salesperson than with what is being sold:

14. *A pleasing personality.* Supersalespeople develop the art of making themselves agreeable to other people. They know that the prospective buyer must buy the salesperson as well as the merchandise or no sale can be made.

15. *Showmanship.* The master salesperson is also a supershowman. The star salesperson reaches the mind of the prospective buyer by dramatizing the presentation and by giving the presentation enough "color" to appeal to the prospective buyer's imagination.

16. *Self-control.* The master salesperson exercises complete control over his or her head and heart at all times. If you don't control yourself, you cannot control your prospective buyer.

17. *Initiative.* The master salesperson understands its value and uses the principle of initiative. They use imagination to create plans that are translated into action through initiative. Salespeople who rise to the top rarely have to be told what to do or how to do it.

18. *Tolerance.* The master salesperson is open-minded and tolerant on all subjects, knowing that open-mindedness is essential for growth.

19. *Accurate thinking.* The master salesperson thinks! If you are going to be a master salesperson you must go to the trouble to gather facts as the basis of your thinking. You should do no guessing when facts are available. You should have no set or immovable opinions that are not based on what you know to be facts.

20. *Persistence.* The master salesperson is never influenced by the word *no* and does not recognize the word *impossible.* The real masters know that all buyers take the line of least resistance by resorting to the "no" excuse. The word *no,* to the master salesperson, is nothing more than a signal to begin the sales presentation in earnest.

21. *Faith.* I do not mean faith in the religious sense. Here the term *faith* refers to that state of mind that may be described as an intense confidence that you can do it. The master salesperson has the capacity for superfaith in:

   • The thing he or she is selling
   • Himself or herself
   • The prospective buyer
   • Closing the sale

   Sales superstars never try to make a sale without having that kind of faith in themselves. They know that faith is contagious, that faith is picked up through the "receiving station" of the prospective buyer's mind and acted upon as if it were that buyer's own state of mind. Without faith there can be no supersalesmanship.

22. *Habit of observation.* The master salesperson is a close observer of small details. Every word uttered by the prospective buyer, every change of facial expression, and every movement is observed and its significance is weighed. The master salesperson not only observes and analyzes accurately what the prospective buyer does and says, but also what the prospective buyer does *not* do or say. Nothing escapes the master salesperson's attention.

23. *The habit of rendering more service than is expected.* The master salesperson follows the habit of rendering service that is greater in quantity and finer in quality than he or she is expected to render. This allows you to profit by the law of increasing returns, as well as by the law of contrast.

24. *Profiting by failures and mistakes.* To the master salesperson there is no such thing as lost effort. He or she profits by their own mistakes and, through observation, by the mistakes of others. In every failure and mistake may be found the seed of an equivalent success.

25. *The Master Mind principle.* Supersalespeople understand and apply the Master Mind principle, through which they greatly multiply their power to achieve. The Master Mind principle means the coordination of two or more individual minds, working in perfect harmony for a definite purpose.

26. *A definite chief aim.* The master salesperson works with a definite sales goal in mind. Masters never go at their work merely with the aim of selling all they can. They not only work with a definite goal in mind, but they have a definite time in which to attain that goal. The psychological effect of a definite chief aim will be described in the chapter on autosuggestion.

27. *The Golden Rule applied.* The master salesperson uses the Golden Rule as the foundation of all business transactions. To be a master salesperson you must be able to put yourself in the other person's shoes and see the situation from your customer's viewpoint.

28. *Enthusiasm.* Of all the qualities that a salesperson must possess, none is more necessary and none more valuable than enthusiasm. The master salesperson has an abundance of enthusiasm which he or she can use at will. Moreover, the true master knows the vibrations of enthusiastic thought that he or she releases will be picked up by the prospective buyer and acted upon as if it were the buyer's own enthusiasm.

HABITS A MASTER SALESPERSON MUST ELIMINATE

Success in selling is the result of positive qualities that you must possess and use. Failure in selling is the result of negative habits that must be eliminated. The following are some of the more outstanding negatives:

1. *The habit of procrastination.* There is no substitute for prompt and persistent action.

2. One or more of the *basic fears.* A salesperson whose mind is filled with any form of fear cannot sell successfully. The six basic fears are:
    *   The fear of poverty
    *   The fear of criticism
    *   The fear of ill health
    *   The fear of loss of love of someone
    *   The fear of old age
    *   The fear of death

3. Spending too much time *making "calls" instead of sales.* A call is not an interview. An interview is not a sale. Some who think they are salespeople have not learned this truth.

4. *Shifting responsibility to the sales manager.* The sales manager is not supposed to go with the salesperson to make calls. Sales managers don't have enough hours or legs to do this. Their business is to tell the salesperson what to do, not to do it for them.

5. Spending too much time and effort *creating excuses.* Explanations do not explain. Orders do. Nothing else does. Don't forget that.

6. Spending too much time in hotel lobbies or any other place the salesperson "parks" to *recoup and regroup.* Do your regrouping on the go. It's too easy to give in to comfortable surroundings.

7. *Buying hard-luck stories* instead of selling merchandise. The economy is a common topic of discussion, but don't let it switch your mind from your own sales presentation.

8. *Partying too hard the night before.* You may have convinced yourself that parties and networking can be good for business, but not if they cut into the following day's business.

9. *Depending on your sales manager for prospects.* Order-takers expect prospective buyers to be hog-tied and held down until they arrive. Master salespeople catch their own prospects. This is one of the chief reasons why they are master salespeople.

10. *Waiting for business conditions to pick up.* This is nothing but an excuse. There is always something that can be done now. It's up to you to find the something.

11. *Fear of the competition, fear of the word "no," and just plain pessimism.* If you start off expecting the customer to say no before you've even knocked on the door, the chances are you won't be disappointed. People can smell fear, and they can spot a loser.

12. *Failure to plan your day in advance.* The person who plans their day in advance also goes about their work logically and efficiently, accomplishing what they have planned to do that day. When there is no organization of schedule, a salesperson literally "does not know where to begin."

13. *Keeping poor records and dates on calls.* Prospects and established customers soon weary of the salesperson who habitually "forgets" to call on specified days. When a customer needs merchandise, they need it then!

14. *Tardiness.* The salesperson who is habitually late for sales meetings, business appointments, and to the office soon finds themself looking for new customers and, often, a new job.

15. *Using dilapidated or out-of-date material.* Crumpled, untidy, and out-of-date materials denote disorganization and a lack of interest on the part of the salesperson.

16. *Being without pen and paper.* A writing instrument is a vital factor to the salesperson's efficiency. The master salesperson invests in a good

pen or pencil that will adequately meet their requirements. They know that prospects quickly tire of the salesperson who always has to borrow something to write with in order to take an order. The customer tires even more quickly of the salesperson who borrows a pen and never gets around to returning it.

17. *Using glasses or adornments as a prop.* Fidgeting with your wristwatch, twirling a ring, or biting the rim of your glasses, as if it helps you to think better, are sure-fire ways to set a customer's nerves on edge and consequently lose a sale.

18. *A tired sales presentation.* Running through your sales presentation as if you were tired of hearing it—singing it out in a monotone and appearing bored with the whole thing—makes your customer or prospect bored with you and your presentation.

19. *Relating personal problems to associates and customers.* Your personal problems are important to you—and only you. Everyone has their share and they don't want to hear about yours.

20. *Failure to read and comply with pertinent material.* Your organization does not produce bulletins or contribute to trade papers to have them made into paper airplanes or thrust into the wastebasket unread. They are produced to tell you something. Read them and keep well-informed.

21. *Discourtesy in parking your car.* The customer who finds a salesperson's car parked in their own allotted parking space is not overly encouraged to buy. Creating a traffic jam by blocking a business driveway is a first-class way to incur the wrath of any prospect and lose the possibility of sales in the future. It's just not that difficult to walk an extra block out of your way.

22. *Promising what your company cannot deliver.* What the salesperson promises, the customer expects to receive. An inability to fulfill a promise is not only embarrassing for the customer and your own company, but is plain bad business.

23. *Being unprepared for rain.* The rain-soaked and soggy salesperson who neglected to prepare for an inevitable rainy day is a sorry sight to the prospect. A light raincoat and umbrella are always invaluable when needed.

24. *Running out of supplies.* The salesperson who is not well-stocked with contracts, brochures, order blanks, and so on often finds themself running as low on sales as on supplies.

25. *Plain pessimism.* The habit of expecting that the prospective buyer will give you the gate is likely to result.

Every supersalesperson knows that every sale is first made to himself or herself. Your fear only exists in your mind. You are only a loser if you think you are. How much you convince yourself determines how much you can convince your buyer.

Study the preceding lists carefully. If you are weak in any of the qualities, you can change that. Selling is an art and a science and may be learned by those with the will to acquire it.

Chapter 2

PEOPLE BUY PERSONALITY

EDITOR'S NOTE

This opening segment combines material from How to Sell Your Way Through Life *with additional material from* Law of Success, *Volume I, Lesson One.*

In any of the great cities of the United States, merchandise of similar nature and price can be found in scores of stores, yet you will find there is always one outstanding store which does more business than any of the others. The reason for this is that behind that store is someone who is paying close attention to the personalities of those who come in contact with the public. People buy personalities as much as merchandise, and it is a question whether they are not influenced more by the personalities with which they come in contact than they are by the merchandise.

It is the personalities behind a business that determine the measure of success the business will enjoy. Modify those personalities so they are more pleasing and more attractive to the patrons of the business, and the business will thrive.

Life insurance has been reduced to such a scientific basis that the cost of insurance does not vary to any great extent, regardless of the company from which you purchase it. Yet, out of the hundreds of life insurance companies doing business, less than a dozen companies do the bulk of the business in the United States.

Why?

Personalities.

Ninety-nine people out of every hundred who purchase life insurance policies do not know what is in their policies and, what is more startling, do not seem to care. What they really purchase is the pleasing personality of some man or woman who knows the value of cultivating such a personality.

Your business in life, or at least the most important part of it, is to achieve success. Success is "the attainment of your desire or definite chief aim without violating the rights of other people." Regardless of what your major aim in life may be, you will attain it with much less difficulty after you learn how to cultivate a pleasing personality and you learn to deal with others without friction or envy.

As I stated earlier, one of the greatest problems of life, if not in fact the greatest, is learning the art of harmonious negotiation with others. You cannot enjoy outstanding success in life without power, and you can never enjoy power without sufficient personality to influence other people to cooperate with you in a spirit of harmony.

This book will show you, step-by-step, how to develop such a personality.

EDITOR'S NOTE

Napoleon Hill placed considerable emphasis on the value of nurturing a pleasing personality, but as you will read, although Hill encourages you to work at changing your personality, it must not be done at the expense of honesty and character. In fact it may have been the issue of character that prompted Hill to write How to Sell Your Way Through Life, *on which this book is based.*

Another high-profile self-help author and lecturer of the day was Dale Carnegie, who, like Hill, had a powerful impact on how business was done. Carnegie's signature book, How to Win Friends and Influence People, *focused on using flattery to present a pleasing personality. This book became especially popular among salespeople.*

Although Dale Carnegie's message had similarities to Napoleon Hill's books, Hill had very specific ideas about the business of selling and salesmanship. Hill was especially critical of the idea of using flattery to influence people to buy what you were selling. Carnegie's reliance upon that basic premise may have been what prompted Hill to go back to his own bestseller, **Law of Success,** *and rewrite his principles of success from the point of view of a salesperson.*

Although he does not directly criticize Dale Carnegie or his book, there is little doubt who or what Hill had in mind when he wrote the following:

To be well-liked gives you great advantages. A pleasing personality is worth a king's ransom to those who possess it, but such a personality is not developed through words of flattery that mean nothing. Every truly great trial lawyer knows that attempts to flatter a jury are always fraught with hazards to the case. The same is true of successful business executives. Self-advancement cannot be built on bluff or flattery. Mere words will never take the place of a practical plan put into action.

Flattery is very often a psychological trick that dishonest people use to lull others into a state of carelessness while they pick their pockets. The human ego is a tricky piece of mental equipment, and flattery is one element to which the ego responds most readily. When anyone starts to flatter you it is a sure indication that person wants some favor or something you possess. Flattery is the chief tool of all con men.

Remember as you read this book that it is not a book on flattery. It is not a book of pleasantries and platitudes. It is not a book on psychological tricks. But it is a book based on the recorded facts and realities of life as they have been organized from experiences of the most able leaders the country has ever produced.

If you want to sell your way through life successfully, look around you, see what useful service you can render to as many people as possible. Make yourself of value to others, and you will not need to learn the art of flattery in order to win people and use personal influence. Moreover, those whom you do win will stay won.

TRUTH IN SELLING

Personally, I resent all attempts by people to flatter me. And I also do not flatter others. I get better results by frankness in my dealings with people, for I find that direct, straight dealing not only wins friends but it tends to hold them.

During the Great Depression of the 1930s, it became apparent to me that being an author at that particular time was not a great business to be in. People were not so interested in books as they were interested in eating!

Like many, I lost all of my money and most of my worldly goods. I closed my New York office and moved to Washington, D.C., where I planned to remain until the economic storm had passed.

Months stretched into years, and instead of the Depression passing, it became worse. Finally I reached a decision not to wait for the end of the business stagnation, but to go on the lecture platform and work my way back into useful service to others who had also been wounded.

I decided to make my start in Washington, and to do it I needed newspaper advertising. The amount of space I required would cost over two thousand dollars and I did not have this amount. I was face to face with a situation that you and every other person on earth must sometime experience. I was in need of something I had to procure with mere words. *[In today's dollars, the value of what Hill needed might be well in excess of $50,000.]*

Here is a brief description of exactly what I did and said in order to solve my problem:

I went to the advertising director of the *Washington Star*, Colonel Leroy Heron. In approaching him I had two courses available to me. I could flatter him; I could tell him what a great paper he represented, what a fine record he made in the World War, what a great advertising man I believed him to be, and all that sort of flattery. Or I could lay my cards on the table and tell him what I wanted, why I wanted it, and why I believed I should get it.

I chose to lay my cards on the table. Then I had to decide whether I would disclose all the facts, including my financial weakness, or skip over these embarrassing subjects without clearly discussing them.

Again I chose to rely upon frankness. As well as I can remember, here is what I said:

"Colonel Heron, I wish to use the *Washington Star* in an advertising campaign to announce a series of public lectures on the philosophy of individual achievement. The space I require will amount to approximately twenty-five hundred dollars. My problem is in the unpleasant fact that I do not have that amount of money available. I did have that much and more, but the Depression has used up my money.

"My request for this credit is not based upon my credit rating. On that basis I would not be entitled to the credit. My appeal is based upon the fact that I have devoted a quarter of a century to the study of the principles of individual achievement. During this time I have had the cooperation of such men as Andrew Carnegie, Thomas A. Edison, John Wanamaker, and Cyrus H. K. Curtis. These men thought enough of me to give freely of their time and experience, over a long period of years, while I was organizing the philosophy of success. The time each gave to me was worth many times the amount of credit I am asking of you. Through their cooperation I am now prepared to take to the world a philosophy of self-help that people badly need. If you do not wish to extend to me the credit as a sound business risk, then extend it in the same spirit of helpfulness in which these men gave me their time and experience."

The credit was extended to me by Colonel Heron, and this is what he said:

"I do not know what are your chances of paying for the space you want, but I know enough of human nature that I believe you honestly intend to pay for the space. I also believe that any philosophy organized from the life work of such men as Edison and Carnegie is sound and needed at this time. Moreover, I believe anyone to whom these men would devote their priceless time is worthy of much more credit than you seek with the *Star*. Bring in your copy and I will run it. We will talk to the credit manager afterward."

How far do you suppose I would have gotten had I appealed to Colonel Heron on anything but frankness?

My analysis of over 30,000 salespeople disclosed the fact that the most common weaknesses in sales presentation were the following:

1. Failure to present a motive for buying
2. Lack of persistence in sales presentation and in closing
3. Failure to qualify prospective buyers
4. Failure to neutralize the minds of prospective buyers
5. Lack of imagination
6. Absence of enthusiasm

Any one of these weaknesses is sufficient to destroy the chances of a sale, but you will note that "failure to present a motive for buying" heads the list.

SELLING AND MOTIVE

There are sound ways of winning friends and influencing people. There are nine windows and doors through which the human mind can be entered and influenced. Not one of these is labeled "flattery." The nine doors are the nine basic motives by which all people are influenced and to which all people respond. These nine motives influence practically every thought and deed, and they are listed in the approximate order of their importance and greatest usefulness:

1. The motive of self-preservation
2. The motive of financial gain
3. The motive of love
4. The motive of sexuality
5. The motive of desire for power and fame
6. The motive of fear
7. The motive of revenge
8. The motive of freedom (of body and mind)
9. The motive of desire to create or build in thought or in material

If you wish to climb to the top of the ladder of success and remain there, it will be much safer to use the nine motives as the rungs of your ladder instead of depending upon flattery.

In order for a customer to purchase your goods or services, that customer must be motivated to buy. To be motivated means that the customer is moved to action by a motive. When the master sales stars qualify prospective buyers, they look first for the most logical motive they may use to influence the buyer's thinking and decision.

Every move, every act, and every thought of every human being is influenced by one or more of the nine basic motives. By mastering, understanding, and applying the nine basic motives, you will learn how to influence people by genuine appeal to natural motives, and you will reduce opposition and friction.

Remember, however, that motive usually must be placed by you in the mind of the prospective buyer. Most people have little inclination to build their own motives to buy what you are selling. Only a weak-willed person will permit themself to be sold unless a sufficiently impelling motive has been tactfully but forcefully planted in his or her mind by the salesperson.

Smart salespeople check their sales presentation against these nine basic motives to make sure that the presentation appeals to as many of the motives as possible. A sales presentation is more effective when based upon more than one motive. If your sales-presentation plan does not emphasize one or more of the nine basic motives, it is weak and should be revised.

No master salesperson will sell anything to anyone without knowing a logical motive for the purchaser to buy. High-pressure methods do not come within the category of master salesmanship. High-pressure sales usually depend upon fast-talking and exaggeration to take the place of motives for buying.

The very fact that high-pressure methods are employed is evidence that the person doing the selling has no logical motive to offer the prospective purchaser as to why he or she should buy. A master at sales would never make that mistake.

PLANTING THE RIGHT MOTIVE

The late Dr. Harper, while serving as president of the University of Chicago, desired to construct a new building on the campus, the estimated cost of which was one million dollars *[at least $20 million today, and probably much more]*. After analysis of the situation, it became apparent to Dr. Harper that he would have to seek the million dollars from an outside source.

Dr. Harper did not start buttonholing wealthy people for donations. He did not put on a drive for donations. He made up his mind to get the entire sum through a single sale. And he personally took on the job of making the sale.

His first move was to lay out a plan of action. His plan involved only two prospective donors. From one or the other he intended to secure the needed funds. His plan was conceived with ingenuity and rounded out with a strategy that was filled with allure! It was also loaded with dynamite. What did he do?

He chose, as his two prospective donors, two Chicago millionaires whom he knew were bitter enemies. One of these men was the head of the Chicago Street Railway system. The other was a politician who had made a fortune by "gouging" the streetcar company.

Yes, yes, I know. You are beginning to see the point before it has been explained. But keep reading to see and appreciate the technique of a master sales artist.

Dr. Harper's selection of prospective buyers of his plan was perfect. This is a point at which all but master artists at selling are usually weak. They do not use sound judgment in the selection of buyers.

After turning his plan over in his mind for a few days, and carefully rehearsing his sales presentation, Dr. Harper swung into action.

Choosing the noon hour as the most favorable for his call, he presented himself at the office of the streetcar magnate. Here was his reason for choosing this particular hour. He calculated that the executive's secretary would be at lunch at that time and that his prospect would be alone in his office. He was right. Finding the outer office empty, he walked on into the private office. The magnate looked up in surprise and asked, "What can I do for you, sir?"

"I beg your pardon," Dr. Harper replied, "I am Dr. Harper, president of the University of Chicago. I found no one in the outer office, so I took the liberty of walking in. I just dropped in to tell you about an idea that has been in my mind for some time. [Here comes the motive. Watch how he plants it in fertile soil.] First of all, I want to tell you how greatly I admire the wonderful streetcar system you have given the people of Chicago. [Neutralizing his prospect's mind.] I believe it to be the greatest system in the country. However, it seems to me that while you have built what should be a great monument to yourself, it is not the kind of thing that people will associate with your name after you are gone. [Watch the master go back now to motive.]

"I had an idea for a monument that will endure forever, but I have run into some opposition which, I am sorry to say, may stand in the way. [Pulling the "lure" away from the prospect to make the idea more desirable.] I had thought of securing for you the privilege of constructing a beautiful granite building on the university campus, but some of the members of our board want this privilege to go to Mr. X [mentioning the name of the political enemy]. I just came by to ask if you can think of any plan that may help me to secure this opportunity for you."

"That is most interesting!" the magnate said. "Please sit down and let's talk about this."

"I am sorry," Dr. Harper replied, "but we are having a board meeting in an hour and if I'm going to get there on time I've got to leave right now. If you think of an argument I can use, please telephone my office. I'll get the message and use it to go to bat for you before the board."

When he reached his office, Dr. Harper found that the streetcar magnate had already called to ask that Dr. Harper phone him as soon as he came in. The doctor telephoned the streetcar man, who requested that he be permitted to present his case to the board in person. Dr. Harper replied that this would be inadvisable; that in view of the opposition some of the board members had expressed toward him, Dr. Harper said that he could present the matter more "diplomatically." (Intensifying the lure.)

The next morning upon arriving at his office, he found the streetcar magnate waiting for him. They were closeted together for half an hour, during which the streetcar magnate assumed the role of salesperson while Dr. Harper became the "buyer" and was "persuaded" to accept a check for a million dollars and to promise that he would try to get it accepted by the board!

The building now stands on the campus of the university, silent but impressive evidence that mastery in selling is never accidental. The building bears the name of the donor.

Let us analyze this transaction to make sure that the fine points are not overlooked. First of all, note that no high-pressure methods were used by Dr. Harper. He depended entirely upon motive to turn the trick for him. No doubt he spent days planning his approach, and he made his appeal through two of the most alluring of all the motives:

1. The motive of desire for fame and power, and

2. The motive of revenge

The streetcar magnate saw instantly that he could perpetuate his name as a public benefactor long after his remains had turned to dust and his streetcar system had, perhaps, been supplanted by some other mode of travel. He saw also (thanks to Dr. Harper's sound strategy) an opportunity to get revenge on his bitterest enemy by depriving him of the privilege of a great honor.

No great amount of imagination is required to see what would have happened if Dr. Harper had made his approach in the usual manner. If Dr. Harper had not understood the psychology of motive and had not been a master salesperson, he would have visited the magnate and this is about the conversation that would have taken place:

"Good morning, sir. I am Dr. Harper, president of the University of Chicago. I have come to ask for a few minutes of your time. [Asking for favors to begin with, instead of offering favors; failure to neutralize the prospective buyer's mind.] We need an extra million dollars for a new building which we intend to erect on the campus of the university, and I thought you might be interested in donating the amount. You have been successful. You have a great street railway system from which you earn big profits made possible through the patronage of the public. Now, it is only fair that you should show your appreciation of the success which the public has made possible for you by doing something for the public good."

Throughout this pitch, the streetcar magnate is fidgeting in his chair, fussing with some papers on his desk, and mentally groping for an excuse with which to refuse. As soon as the doctor hesitates for a moment in his sales pitch, the magnate takes up the conversation.

"I am very sorry, Dr. Harper, but our budget for philanthropic purposes has been entirely exhausted. You know we make a liberal annual donation to the Community Chest fund. There is nothing more we can do this year. Besides, a million dollars is a large sum of money. I am sure our board could not be persuaded to donate so much money to charity."

That word—*charity*. Dr. Harper would now be in the unhappy position of one who begs for charity. Giving to charity, as such, is not listed as one of the nine basic motives that move people to action. But lift the word *charity* out of its humble setting and give it the color of privilege, fame, and honor, and it takes on an entirely different meaning. Only a master salesperson can do this.

One way is clever; the other is crude.

Motive is the seed from which big sales grow. A seed must contain the life germ or it will not germinate, regardless of the kind of soil in which it is planted. Similarly, motive must contain the life germ or it will not germinate into a sale. When an appropriate motive has been planted in the mind of the prospective buyer, it begins to work from within, as yeast works in a loaf of bread. The person who understands how to inject the germ of life into motive is a master salesperson—a master because he or she captures the prospective buyer's own imagination and makes it work to the salesperson's advantage.

Chapter 3

AUTOSUGGESTION

———————

EDITOR'S NOTE

Napoleon Hill's approach to selling is not simply a bag full of tricks-of-the-trade and a collection of pitches or scripts to be memorized. He was most interested in teaching the psychology of selling, and the basic technique that underlies all of Hill's principles of success is in fact a psychological tool It is the use of autosuggestion as a way of altering your habits and beliefs so that you can make yourself into the master salesperson you want to become.

Because autosuggestion plays a significant role in each of the follow-ing chapters, Napoleon Hill devoted this chapter to the theory behind autosuggestion and the ways in which you can use the technique. This first section, adapted from **The Success System That Never Fails,** *will provide a clear understanding of the terminology.*

Suggestion comes from the outside. It is anything you see, hear, feel, taste, or smell. If I say to you, "Try to do the right thing because it is right," that is a suggestion from me to you.

Self-suggestion is purposefully controlled from within. It is a suggestion you give to yourself. You can see it in your imagination, say it to yourself, or write it down. Each time you think or say to yourself, "Try to do the right thing because it is right," that is self-suggestion.

Autosuggestion acts by itself, unconsciously, like a machine that reacts in the same way from the same stimulus. Each time your subconscious flashes to your conscious mind "Try to do the right thing because it is right," that is autosuggestion.

If, during the next week, every morning and every evening and frequently throughout the day you repeat the phrase, "Try to do the right thing because it is right," when you are faced with temptation, that self-motivator will flash from your subconscious to your conscious mind. In this way, through repetition, you will form a habit—a good habit— that will help make your future a success.

EDITOR'S NOTE

In **How to Sell Your Way Through Life,** *Napoleon Hill discusses the theory and practice of the two most common methods of using auto-suggestion: positive affirmations and creative visualization. He begins by explaining the use of positive affirmations.*

SELLING YOURSELF ON YOURSELF

Autosuggestion is self-motivation. It is the principle through which you impress upon your subconscious mind an idea, plan, concept, or belief. Repetition of positive suggestions to your subconscious mind is the most effective way of educating it to broadcast only positive messages.

If you have ever noticed how, without saying a word, your enthusiasm or lack of enthusiasm can influence others, then you know that in some way your subconscious mind is like a broadcasting station that sends your thoughts and beliefs (or disbeliefs) to others. If you are aware of this, and if you are a master salesperson, you should realize that before you can successfully sell to someone else, you must first educate your subconscious mind to broadcast your belief in what you offer for sale.

One of the most effective ways to influence your subconscious mind is through the use of positive affirmations. A positive affirmation is a short phrase that clearly states the change you want to make in yourself. If you charge that phrase with total faith and belief that you are capable of changing yourself, and if you repeat the phrase over and over to yourself until thinking that way becomes your natural habit, then you will make the change you desire.

EDITOR'S NOTE

The following is adapted from material in **Think and Grow Rich: The 21st-Century Edition:**

The affirmation that most people are familiar with is "Every day, in every way, I am getting better and better." It was devised by the noted French psychologist Emile Coué, a contemporary of Sigmund Freud who operated a clinic for patients diagnosed with psychosomatic ailments (individuals who have convinced themselves they are ill, and even show symptoms, but do not actually have a disease).

Dr. Coué used autosuggestion techniques with his patients, and as part of his treatment he developed this general, nonspecific phrase that anyone could use. It would give the subconscious a positive instruction, but was open enough that it did not tell the subconscious a specific problem to deal with, nor did it try to tell the subconscious how to do it. When Coué instructed his patients to repeat the positive-affirmation phrase "Every day, in every way, I am getting better and better" several times a day, improvements among his patients happened so quickly and dramatically that his method became the talk of medical and scientific circles. The use of the phrase practically became a movement in turn-of-the-century Europe.

Affirmations can be an effective autosuggestion tool for changing habits and beliefs because of certain characteristics of the conscious and unconscious mind.

The Conscious Mind: Your conscious mind receives information through the five senses of sight, smell, taste, hearing, and touch. Your conscious mind keeps track of what you need for thinking and operating, and it filters out what you don't need. Your conscious mind (and what your memory retains) is the intelligence with which you normally think, reason, and plan.

The Subconscious Mind: Your subconscious has access to all the same information your conscious mind receives, but it doesn't reason the way your conscious mind does. It takes everything literally. It doesn't make value judgments. It does not filter or interpret, it simply processes information literally and stores it.

Habits and Beliefs: Because the subconscious mind does not distinguish between what is real and what is vividly imagined, if you convincingly plant an idea in your subconscious, it will accept the idea as though it were a fact. If you have planted the new idea strongly enough, when your thoughts run in that direction your new idea will be the first thought that comes to mind. It will have become your new belief, and eventually it will be your habit.

For those readers who may be dubious about the subconscious, or that thoughts stored below the level of consciousness can exert enough influence to affect attitude and behavior, the following explanation should help alleviate such doubts.

There is no doubt about the existence of the conditions known by the psychological terms fixations, phobias, and compulsive behaviors. These conditions often occur when a child has learned something in such a powerful or dramatic way that the knowledge becomes firmly planted in the child's subconscious mind. Then, even as the child grows to adulthood and the conscious mind learns to understand that information from a mature point of view, because the childhood learning experience was so powerful, the subconscious still retains the childhood understanding of the information. It was so emotionalized that it overrides the adult's logical, conscious mind.

It is a fact that a traumatic experience—the result of which creates a strongly planted idea—can influence the way a person thinks and acts. Therefore, by intentionally using all of your efforts to powerfully plant a positive idea in your subconscious, you will be creating what would amount to a "good" traumatic experience that will influence the way you think and act, in a positive way.

If you do everything within your power to strongly, firmly, and with complete faith and conviction, plant the idea that you will be successful and achieve your desire, your subconscious will accept and store that idea. If you have planted the idea so strongly that it is the dominant idea in your subconscious, it will influence all of the other ideas and information stored there.

Your subconscious will not judge if it is true or false, positive or negative, but it does respond to the power of the input (how emotionalized the thought is).

The following resumes from **How to Sell Your Way Through Life.**

USE POSITIVE EMOTIONS TO SELL OTHERS

Cold reasoning has no influence whatsoever on the subconscious mind. The subconscious responds only to the impulses of thought that have been emotionalized or mixed with strong feelings.

The world is controlled by emotions. Most of our activities, from birth until death, are induced by our feelings. The salesperson who can appeal to the buyer's emotions or feelings will make ten sales for every one made by the salesperson who appeals to buyers through their reason alone. Buyers generally make purchases because of some motive closely associated to their emotions.

THE SEVEN MAJOR POSITIVE EMOTIONS

1. The emotions related to sex
2. The emotion of love
3. The emotion of hope

4. The emotion of faith

5. The emotion of enthusiasm

6. The emotion of optimism

7. The emotion of loyalty

You must mix one or more of these positive emotions with the suggestions you plant in your subconscious mind if you want to broadcast thoughts and feelings that will influence your potential buyer in your favor.

AVOID NEGATIVE EMOTIONS

As you will recall, it was stated that the subconscious is influenced when the ideas are strongly emotionalized, but it does not differentiate between emotions that are positive or negative. The subconscious mind responds to the intensity of the emotion, not the kind of emotion. Your subconscious is influenced by the negatives just as readily as it is by the positives.

THE SEVEN MAJOR NEGATIVE EMOTIONS

1. The emotion of anger (quick and transitory)

2. The emotion of fear (prominent and easily discernible)

3. The emotion of greed (subtle and persistent)

4. The emotion of jealousy (impulsive and spasmodic)

5. The emotion of revenge (subtle and quiet)

6. The emotion of hatred (subtle and persistent)

7. The emotion of superstition (subtle and slow)

The presence of these negative emotional impulses in the mind will almost always overcome the positive emotions. Any positive suggestion you try to plant in your subconscious mind, while one or more of these negative emotions is present, will be colored by the negative. When the subconscious mind broadcasts such mixed suggestions it will register a negative result in the minds of those who pick up the vibration.

EDITOR'S NOTE

Adapted from Think and Grow Rich: The 21st-Century Edition:

Napoleon Hill's concern about the susceptibility of the subconscious mind to negative thoughts, emotions, and comments is well known to professionals who work with these techniques. In clinical hypnotherapy there is an axiom referred to as the law of reversed effect, which states that whenever there is a conflict between imagination and willpower, the imagination wins. When you attempt to plant an idea, if the subconscious already harbors a negative, trying to force the new idea has the reverse effect because the subconscious becomes obsessed with defending its established negative idea. And the harder you "try" to do something, the more the subconscious resists and the more difficult it becomes.

Even the use of the word "try" is warned against because it gives the suggestion to the subconscious of a preconceived failure. The concept of "trying" implies an ongoing effort. You don't want to try; you want to succeed. If you ask your subconscious to help you "try," it may do just that. It may help you try, but it will prevent you from succeeding—because if you did succeed, then it could no longer help you "try," which is what you asked it to do.

This cautionary note about using the word "try" is just one example of the care that should be taken when formulating affirmations and using autosuggestion.

The following are some rules of thumb that most modern experts agree are important when creating affirmations.

1. *Affirmations should always be stated as a positive. Affirm what you do want, not what you don't want.*

2. *Affirmations work best when they are short and very clear about a single desired goal. Take the time to write, rewrite, and polish your affirmation until you can express your desire in a short statement of precise and well-chosen words.*

3. *Affirmations should be specific about the desired goal, but not about how to accomplish it. Your subconscious knows better than you what it can do and how it can do it.*

4. *Do not make unreasonable time demands. Your subconscious can't make anything happen "suddenly" or "now."*

5. *Just saying the words will have little effect. When you affirm your desire you must do it with such faith and conviction that your subconscious becomes convinced of how important it is to you. As you affirm your desire to yourself, visualize it in your mind's eye as big as a billboard. Make it big, powerful, and memorable.*

6. *Repetition of your emotionalized affirmation is crucial. At this time it is your habit to think one way. By repeating your affirmation often, every day, your new way of thinking will begin to be your automatic response. Keep reinforcing it until it becomes second nature to you and your habit will have become to think the new way—the way you want to think.*

If you seriously commit yourself to doing these things, it will change the way you think and act. When you have given your subconscious a specific direction that it did not have before, it will begin to put together pieces of information and you will find that you are coming up with more and better plans and ideas to accomplish your goal.

Your subconscious will do everything it can to transmute your desire into reality, and because of the enthusiasm that radiates from you, other people will want to do what they can to help you succeed.

The following resumes the material adapted from **How to Sell Your Way Through Life**.

DON'T EVEN THINK NEGATIVE THOUGHTS

Feelings, beliefs, and thoughts released by the salesperson, through his or her subconscious mind, often speak more loudly than words. If you understand this principle, you will know why you must sell yourself first, before trying to sell others. This also explains why the negative-minded salesperson hears the "no" so often.

Politics and politicians command little respect today. Analyze the brand of salesmanship used by politicians and you will easily understand why they have lost the confidence of their "buyers." Every campaign runs negative ads attacking their opponent, instead of selling themselves to the voters on their own merit.

No well-managed business would ever permit salespeople to seek customers by knocking competitors. Sales managers know that sales made by belittling competitors or competitive merchandise are not really sales, and that business obtained in this way is a liability in the long run.

Out-and-out statements of a negative nature are the equivalent of suicide in selling. Negative statements in selling not only set up resentment in the mind of the prospective buyer, but they also infect the salesperson's own subconscious mind so that it throws off negative vibrations that are picked up by other people and acted upon to the detriment of the salesperson.

Satire, sarcasm, and innuendo may give a salesperson a reputation as being quick with a one-liner, but that kind of negativism will not help him or her sell products.

The master salesperson doesn't speak negative words or allow his or her subconscious mind to broadcast negative thoughts. Like attracts like. Negative suggestions attract negative action and negative decisions from prospective purchasers.

Remember that people are motivated to buy or not to buy, through their feelings. Much of what they believe to be their own feelings consist of thought impulses they have unconsciously picked up from the messages sent out by the salesperson.

EDITOR'S NOTE

The use of autosuggestion to bolster confidence in the product or service you are offering for sale can be a very valuable selling tool, but even more valuable is the way in which autosuggestion can be used to change your habits.

In this context, the habits Napoleon Hill refers to are not habits such as smoking, overeating, or bad posture. Here, Hill is dealing with aspects of your character and personality that have become habits, such as your self-confidence, enthusiasm, initiative, and persistence. When you change these habits, you make profound changes that will have a major influence on everything you do and how successful you will be.

HOW TO FORM HABITS

[The following is adapted from **Law of Success**, *Volume III, Lesson Twelve.]*

There is a close relationship between habit and autosuggestion. Through habit, an act repeatedly performed in the same manner has a tendency to become permanent, and eventually we come to perform the act automatically or unconsciously. In playing a piano, for example, the artist can play a familiar piece while his or her conscious mind is on some other subject.

We form habits based on the degree of reinforcement we receive. Habits make no moral judgments; they can be either good or bad. Both are formed through repetition. If we try something and like the results, we repeat the action. You can replace negative thoughts with positive ones, you can replace inaction with action, and you can form any habit you choose. Your thoughts are the only thing in life that you can completely control—if you choose to do so. You can control your thoughts to control your habits.

Autosuggestion is the tool with which we dig a mental path, concentration is the hand that holds that tool, and habit is the map or blueprint that the mental path follows. An idea or desire, to be transformed into terms of action or physical reality, must be held in the conscious mind faithfully and persistently until habit begins to give it permanent form.

The following are the rules through which you may form the habits you desire:

I. At the beginning of the formation of a new habit, put force and enthusiasm into expressing what you want to become. Feel what you think. Remember that you are taking the first steps toward making your new mental paths, and it is much harder at first than it will be afterward. At the beginning, make each path as clear and as deep as you can, so that you can readily see it the next time you wish to follow it.

2. Keep your attention firmly concentrated on your new path-building and forget all about the old paths. Concern yourself only with the new ones that you are building to order.

3. Travel over your newly made paths as often as possible. Create opportunities for doing so, without waiting for them to arise through luck or chance. The more often you go over the new paths, the sooner they will become well-worn and easily traveled.

4. Resist the temptation to travel over the older, easier paths you have been using in the past. Every time you resist a temptation, the stronger you become and the easier it will be for you to do so the next time. But every time you yield to the temptation, the easier it becomes to yield again and the more difficult it becomes to resist the next time. This is the critical time. Prove your determination, persistency, and willpower now, at the very beginning.

5. Be sure you have mapped out the right path as your goal or aim, then go ahead without fear and without allowing yourself to doubt. Select your goal and make good, deep, wide mental paths leading straight to it.

EDITOR'S NOTE

The preceding explains generally what to do to create new habits. The following explains specifically how to do it using the second method of autosuggestion. Napoleon Hill refers to this method as concentration, but today it is most often called creative visualization, and it is the autosuggestion technique widely taught by contemporary motivational experts. Creative visualization is also used by some of the most successful trainers of Olympic athletes and professional sports teams, it is used by NASA in training astronauts, and medical professionals use it in a variety of ways including teaching it to patients who need to elevate their autoimmune system.

Virtually every newspaper, magazine, and television news program regularly features stories on the crucial role the mind plays in personal growth and achievement. Techniques based on autosuggestion have fostered countless bestselling books, audiobooks, and video programs, and on the Internet there are over two million Web links mentioning visualization techniques. Every week thousands of people attend seminars, lectures, and retreats to be inspired by motivational speakers or spiritual leaders and to learn techniques that will help them achieve success —almost all of which are based on the principles Napoleon Hill writes about in this book.

The following is from adaptations of material from **Think and Grow Rich: The 21ˢᵗ-Century Edition** *and* **How to Sell Your Way Through Life.**

CONCENTRATION IS VISUALIZATION

Concentration, as it is used in this book, is defined as "the habit of planting in the mind a definite aim, objective, or purpose, and visualizing that objective until ways and means for its realization have been created." Concentration is the principle through which you may build your habits to order.

Habits are formed step-by-step through our every thought and deed. Either you control your habits or your habits will control you. If you are going to be successful, you will force yourself to build only the kind of habits that you are willing to let control you. "We first make our habits, and our habits then make us."

The principle of habit and the principle of concentration go hand in glove. Habit may grow out of concentration, and concentration may grow out of habit. The object of concentrating upon a definite aim is to train the mind until it forms the habit of focusing upon that aim. When focusing on your aim becomes a habit, then your subconscious is constantly influenced to pick up the concept of that aim and to translate it into its physical counterpart. And your subconscious will try to do that through the most practical and direct methods available.

Concentration in salesmanship means planting in your conscious mind a definite chief aim, idea, plan, or purpose and the continuous focusing upon it of the conscious mind. It means the ability to control your attention and focus it on a given problem until you have solved that problem. It means the ability to throw off the effects of the habits you wish to discard, and the power to build new habits. It means complete self-mastery.

Concentration is the ability to think as you wish to think, the ability to control your thoughts and direct them to a definite end, and the ability to organize your knowledge into a plan of action that is sound and workable.

The principle of concentration is the way in which procrastination is overcome. It is the foundation upon which both self-confidence and self-control are predicated.

Ambition and desire are the major factors that enter into the act of successful concentration. If your goal or desire is within reason and it is strong enough, the magic key of concentration will help you attain it.

Nothing was ever created by a human being that was not first created in the imagination, through desire, and then transformed into reality through concentration.

EDITOR'S NOTE

[Adapted from **Think and Grow Rich: The 21st-Century Edition.***]*

It is an axiom of contemporary motivation theory that the subconscious mind cannot distinguish between what is real and what is vividly imagined. One of the most frequently cited studies supporting this concept was done with a group of basketball players. The players were divided into three teams and the players on each team were tested on their ability to make free throws. The teams were then separated for a period of time and each team was given instructions which they were told would improve their abilities. One team was instructed to practice making baskets on a daily basis. The second team was instructed not to practice during the period and not to even think about basketball. The third team was also

*instructed not to practice during the period, but instead the members
were told to spend their daily practice time visualizing in detail the process
of making baskets.*

*At the end of the experiment the teams were again tested. The
team that rested showed a decrease in ability. The team that practiced
showed a marked increase in ability. And the team that didn't practice
but visualized making baskets showed an increase in ability almost equal
to those who had practiced daily.*

*As Hill says, you can "deceive" your subconscious through auto-
suggestion. If you convincingly plant an idea in your subconscious, your
subconscious will accept and work with the idea as though it were a
fact. Thoughts do remain stored in the subconscious. They remain just
as they were when they were input, and the more highly emotionalized
the thoughts are when they are input, the more influence they exert
on attitude and behavior. It is this aspect of the subconscious that
will allow you to use autosuggestion as a tool with which to input the
positive thoughts that will help you achieve the success you desire.*

INSTRUCTIONS FOR APPLYING CONCENTRATION

[Compiled from materials excerpted and adapted from **How to Sell Your
Way Through Life** *and* **Law of Success,** *Volume III, Lesson Twelve.]*

1. Master and apply the principles of autosuggestion by giving orders
   to your subconscious mind, mixing your thoughts with one or more
   of the positive emotions and repeating your orders over and over.

2. Empty your conscious mind of all other thoughts. After a little
   practice you will be able to focus your mind entirely upon any
   subject that you please. The act of focusing on one subject and
   keeping your mind on that one subject is concentration.

3. Hold your thoughts to the object of your concentration with a
   burning desire for the attainment of whatever aim you have in mind.
   When concentrating upon your definite chief aim, you should have
   complete faith that you will realize that goal.

4. When you find your conscious mind wandering, drive it back and focus it upon that subject again and again until you have developed such perfect self-control that you can keep all other thoughts out of your mind. Mix emotion with your thoughts when concentrating; otherwise they will not penetrate to your subconscious mind.

5. The principle of concentration is best practiced when you are in an environment of silence where there are no distractions or disturbances.

6. Your subconscious mind can best be reached and influenced when you concentrate in your conscious mind upon an idea, plan, or purpose in a spirit of intense enthusiasm. Enthusiasm will arouse your creative imagination and put it into action.

Now, let us go back to the starting point. If you choose to, you can throw off any bad influences from your past and build your own life the way you want it to be. You will become what you want to be because of the dominating thoughts that you permit to occupy your mind.

How can the original seed of an idea, plan, purpose, or sales objective be planted in the mind? The answer: Any idea, plan, purpose, or goal may be placed in the mind through the repetition of visualizations of your desire. This is why you are instructed to write out a statement of your desire, purpose, goal, or sales objective, commit it to memory, and repeat it aloud, day after day, until these vibrations of sound have reached your subconscious mind.

1. To begin the creative visualization process, write out a clear, concise statement of the amount of money you intend to acquire. Fix in your mind the exact amount that you desire. It is not sufficient merely to say, "I want plenty of money." Be definite about the amount. (There is a psychological reason for such definiteness.)

2. Determine exactly what you intend to give in return for the money you desire. (There is no such reality as "something for nothing.")

3. Set a definite date when you intend to possess the money you desire.

4. Create a definite plan for carrying out your desire and begin at once, whether you are ready or not, to put this plan into action. For example, suppose that as a general sales goal you intend to accumulate $50,000 by the first of January, five years from now, and that you intend to give your personal services as a salesperson in return for the money. Your written statement of your purpose should be similar to the following:

By the first day of January, _____ [enter year], I will have in my possession $50,000, which will come to me in various amounts from time to time during the interim.

In return for this money I will give the most efficient service of which I am capable. I will give the fullest possible quantity and the best possible quality of service as a salesperson of _____ [describe the service or merchandise you intend to sell].

I believe that I will have this money in my possession. My faith is so strong that I can now see this money before my eyes. I can touch it with my hands. It is now awaiting transfer to me at the time and in the proportion that I deliver the service in return for it. I am awaiting a plan for getting this money, and I will follow that plan when it is received.

Signed . . . .

Read this statement aloud at least twice daily. Go to a quiet spot where you will not be disturbed or interrupted. Close your eyes and repeat aloud (so that you may hear your own words) the written statement of the amount of money you intend to accumulate. Read it once before retiring at night, and once after arising in the morning. As you read, see, feel, and believe yourself already in possession of the money.

When you concentrate on your aim or desire, visualize yourself as you will be; look ahead one, three, five, or even ten years. See, in your imagination, yourself in possession of the money you wish to receive. See yourself in your own home that you have purchased with the proceeds from your efforts as the salesperson you wish to be. See yourself in possession of a nice bank account for your retirement. See yourself as a person of influence, due to your great ability to sell yourself. See yourself engaged in a life-calling in which you will not fear the loss of your position.

Paint this picture clearly, through the powers of your imagination, and it will soon become transformed into a picture of deeply seated desire.

When you begin to "fix in your own mind the exact amount of money you desire," close your eyes and hold your thoughts on that amount of money until you can actually see the physical appearance of it. Do this at least once each day.

You may think it is impossible for you to "see yourself in possession of money" before you actually have it. Here is where a burning desire will come to your aid. If you truly desire your goal so keenly that your desire is an obsession, you will have no difficulty in convincing yourself that you will acquire it.

Make yourself believe that you must have the amount of money you are visualizing. Make your subconscious believe that this money is already awaiting your claim, so your subconscious mind must hand over to you practical plans for acquiring the money that is yours.

When visualizing the money you intend to accumulate, see yourself rendering the service or delivering the merchandise you intend to give in return for this money.

In the fourth step you were instructed to "create a definite plan for carrying out your desire and begin at once to put this plan into action." Do not trust to your "reason" when creating your plan for accumulating money. Just start right now to see yourself in possession of the money, demanding and expecting that your subconscious mind will hand over the plans you need. When the plans appear, they will probably "flash" into your mind in the form of an inspiration or intuition.

Do not become discouraged if you cannot control and direct your emotions the first time you try. Remember, there is no such possibility as something for nothing. You cannot cheat, even if you desire to do so. The price of ability to influence your subconscious mind is persistence in applying the principles described here. You, and you alone, must decide whether or not the reward (the money-consciousness) is worth the price you must pay for it in effort.

Your ability to use the autosuggestion technique of creative visualization will depend, very largely, upon your capacity to concentrate on and clearly visualize a given desire until that desire becomes a burning obsession.

EDITOR'S NOTE

Using visualization effectively is much more than simply daydreaming. Because readers may find that they have difficulty achieving the kind of vivid imagery that is required for it to produce results, the editors offer the following list of books which are particularly helpful in developing the technique of creating powerful mental imagery. Most are also available on audio: Visualization: Directing the Movies of Your Mind *by Adelaide Bry;* Creative Visualization *by Shakti Gawain;* Psycho-Cybernetics *by Dr. Maxwell Maltz;* The Initiation *by Donald Schnell, which includes a description of the visualization technique in spiritual story form; and the collection of audiobooks featuring Silva Method trainer Hans DeJong, which includes an unusual method of quieting the mind using an audio tone that is designed to put the mind in the alpha state.*

INFINITE INTELLIGENCE

[The final section of this chapter is adapted from Law of Success, *Volume III, Lesson Eleven, with additional material from* How to Sell Your Way Through Life.*]*

The camera makes a perfect allegory for the process of creative visualization. First comes the selection of the object to be exposed before the camera. This represents your chief aim, or your goal, or the aspect of your character that you wish to change. Then comes the actual operation of recording that purpose, through the lens of auto-suggestion, onto the subconscious mind.

The part that you must play is clear. You select the picture to be recorded (your definite chief aim, your desire, your definiteness of purpose). Then you focus your conscious mind on this goal or purpose with such intensity that it communicates with the subconscious mind, through autosuggestion, and registers the picture. You then begin to watch for and to expect manifestations of physical realization of the subject of that picture.

Any idea, plan, purpose, or definite aim that you persistently submit to your subconscious mind through concentration will bring to your aid an unexplainable and intangible force that I have termed infinite intelligence. Through infinite intelligence, new ideas and plans will begin to flash into your mind.

EDITOR'S NOTE

Napoleon Hill uses the term **infinite intelligence** *to identify the part of the human mind and thinking process that produces hunches, intuitions, and foresight. Infinite intelligence also describes the thinking process that takes bits of information and ideas that our conscious mind has filtered out or forgotten, and connects them with each other on a subconscious level to create a new idea, which comes to us as a leap of logic or a flash of inspiration.*

When you first start your practice of concentration, do not expect infinite intelligence to move quickly on your behalf. You did not walk the first time you tried, but as you matured walking became habit and you did it without effort. As you become more adept in the use of the principle of autosuggestion, and as your faith and understanding grow, you will see that what you have visualized is beginning to be translated into physical reality.

Bear in mind that you do not go to bed and sleep, with the expectation of awaking to find that infinite intelligence has showered you with the object of your desire or goal. You must work to make it happen —with full faith and confidence that natural ways and means for the attainment of the object of your definite purpose will open to you at the proper time and in a suitable manner.

Infinite intelligence will not command your bank to place money in your account, just because you suggested this to your subconscious mind. But infinite intelligence will open to you the way in which you may earn or borrow that money and place it in your account yourself.

In short, do not rely on miracles for the attainment of the object of your visualization. However, you can rely on the power of infinite intelligence to help direct you, through natural channels, toward its attainment.

I am fully aware that much of what I am proposing will not be believed by the beginner. I remember my own experiences at the start. Skepticism, in connection with all new ideas, is characteristic of all human beings. If you follow the instructions, your skepticism will soon be replaced by belief. And belief will become crystallized into absolute faith in your ability.

Chapter 4

A DEFINITE CHIEF AIM

Every successful person follows five fundamental steps to success. Some follow it unconsciously or by accident, while others follow it with a definite purpose and by design. If you are reading this book, you are already on the path to following the program intentionally. The five fundamental steps that must be taken by all who succeed are:

1. Choice of a definite goal to be attained
2. Development of sufficient power to attain your goal
3. Perfection of a practical plan for attaining your goal
4. Accumulation of specialized knowledge necessary for the attainment of your goal
5. Persistence in carrying out the plan

EDITOR'S NOTE

When Napoleon Hill wrote the original edition of **Law of Success**, *the first of his seventeen principles of success was entitled A Definite Chief Aim. When he wrote* **Think and Grow Rich**, *he renamed it Desire. In* *other works he called it Definiteness of Purpose. These three different names described a concept that encompasses what most contemporary motivational writers refer to as goal-setting.*

As it is used today, goal-setting tends to refer to individual sales goals and is very often considered an offshoot of time management. However, as Napoleon Hill envisioned it, the concept not only applies to setting individual goals on a project-by-project basis, but it also encompasses committing to larger life-goals. As Hill uses it, your desire or definite chief aim could be as big as launching a national marketing campaign, as all-encompassing as deciding on your future profession, or it could be as small as convincing one other person of your idea or opinion. The techniques taught in the chapter on autosuggestion apply equally to big or small.

The following explanation is adapted from the Napoleon Hill Foundation's book **Believe and Achieve.**

Your desire, chief goal, or definiteness of purpose is more than goal-setting. In simplest terms, your desire or purpose is your road map to achieving an overall career objective. The individual goals that represent specific steps along the way are also desires or purposes.

Having a desire or definiteness of purpose for your life has a synergistic effect on your ability to achieve your goals. As you become better at what you do, you devote all of your resources toward reaching your objective, you become more alert to opportunities, and you reach decisions more quickly. Every action you take ultimately boils down to the question: Will this goal help me reach my desire, my overall objective, or won't it?

Your purpose will become your life; it will permeate your mind, both conscious and subconscious. The object of your definite chief aim should become your hobby. You should ride this hobby continuously. You should sleep with it, eat with it, play with it, work with it, live with it, and think with it.

Whatever you want you may get—if you want it with sufficient intensity and keep on wanting it, providing the object wanted is one within reason and you actually believe you will get it. There is a difference, however, between merely wishing for something and actually believing you will get it. A lack of understanding of this difference has meant failure to millions of people.

THE ADVANTAGES OF A DEFINITE AIM

Working with definiteness of purpose toward a single goal has many advantages, among them the following:

1. Singleness of purpose forces you to specialize, and specialization tends toward perfection.

2. A definite goal permits you to develop the capacity to reach decisions quickly and firmly.

3. Definiteness of purpose enables you to master the habit of procrastination.

4. Definiteness of purpose saves the time and energy you would otherwise waste while wavering between two or more possible courses of action.

5. A definite purpose serves as a roadmap which charts the direct route to the end of your journey.

6. Definiteness of purpose fixes your habits so that they are taken over by the subconscious mind and used as a motivating force (involuntarily) in driving toward your goal.

7. Definiteness of purpose develops self-confidence and attracts the confidence of other people.

Laboring will earn you a daily wage. The price of labor has a fixed price that is determined by the law of supply and demand.

Brains, when marketed through a definite aim, have no fixed price. The sky is the limit in the marketing of specialized talent.

These are statements of obvious fact, yet ninety-eight out of every hundred people fail all through life because they do not follow the principle of working with definiteness of purpose.

Those who know where they are going usually get there. They do not waste their time and energy trying to accomplish too many goals at once, nor do they bounce from one desire to the next, quickly abandoning anything that doesn't bring immediate satisfaction. They concentrate their efforts on a definite objective, exerting all powers to attain that end. When it is accomplished they reset their sights and move on to another desire or goal. However, if, after giving serious effort, it becomes apparent that your desire cannot be accomplished, you change your desire or goal, and put all of your focus and energy into that.

DO WHAT YOU LOVE

[The following section is adapted from material excerpted from **Law of Success,** *Volume I, Lesson Two.]*

In your search for the work for which you are best suited, bear in mind that you will most likely attain the greatest success by finding out what work you like best. It is a fact that people who have the greatest success are those who have found work into which they can throw their whole heart and soul. Search until you find out what your particular line of endeavor will be, make it the object of your definite chief aim, and then organize all of your forces and attack it with the belief that you are going to win.

When you choose a definite purpose and make up your mind that you will carry out that purpose, from the very moment that you make the choice, your purpose becomes the dominating thought in your consciousness. From the time that you plant a definite purpose in your mind, your mind begins, both consciously and unconsciously, to gather and store away the material with which you are to accomplish that purpose. You are constantly on the alert for facts, information, and knowledge with which to achieve that purpose.

Desire is the factor that determines what your definite purpose in life shall be. No one can select your dominating desire for you, but once you select it yourself it becomes your definite chief aim and occupies the spotlight of your mind until it is transformed into reality, unless you permit it to be pushed aside by conflicting desires.

Science has established that through the principle of autosuggestion any deeply rooted desire saturates the entire body and mind with the nature of that desire. It then transforms the mind into a powerful magnet that will attract the object of the desire, if it is within reason.

As I said in the chapter on autosuggestion, merely desiring an automobile will not cause the automobile to come rolling in. But if there is a burning desire for an automobile, that desire will lead to the appropriate action through which an automobile may be paid for.

YOUR ENVIRONMENT INFLUENCES YOUR HABITS

The subconscious mind may be likened to a magnet; when it has been charged with any definite purpose, it has a decided tendency to attract all that is necessary for the fulfillment of that purpose. Like attracts like, and you may see evidence of this law in every blade of grass and every growing tree. The acorn attracts from the soil and the air the necessary materials out of which to grow an oak tree. It never grows a tree that is part oak and part poplar.

Every grain of wheat that is planted in the soil attracts the materials out of which to grow a stalk of wheat. It never makes a mistake and grows both oats and wheat on the same stalk.

People, too, are subject to this same law of attraction. Go into any inexpensive boardinghouse district in any city and there you will find a certain kind of person. Go into any prosperous community and there you will find other kinds of persons associated together. Those who are successful seek the company of others who are successful; those who are on the ragged side of life seek the company of those who are in similar circumstances.

All of which leads up to this: You will attract to you people who harmonize with your own philosophy of life, whether you wish it or not. For this reason it is very important that you fill your mind with a definite chief aim that will attract to you people and circumstances that will be of help to you and not a hindrance.

We absorb the material for thought from our surrounding environment. What I mean by the term *environment* covers a very broad field. It consists of the books we read, the people with whom we associate, the country and community in which we live, the nature of the work we do, the clothes we wear, the songs we sing, and, most important of all, the religious and intellectual training we receive in our early teenage years.

The purpose of analyzing the subject of environment is to show its direct relationship to the personality you are developing, and how its influence will give you the materials out of which you may attain your definite chief aim in life.

The first step is to create in your own mind a clear, well-defined picture of the environment in which you believe you could best attain your definite chief aim. Then concentrate your mind on this picture until you transform it into reality.

The mind feeds upon that which we supply it, or that which is forced upon it, through our environment. Therefore, let us select our environment, as much as possible, with the object of supplying the mind with suitable material out of which to carry on its work. If your environment is not to your liking, change it.

Your daily associates constitute one of the most important and influential parts of your environment, and may work for your progress or against it. As much as possible, you should select as your closest daily associates those who are in sympathy with your aims and ideals —especially those represented by your definite chief aim.

You should make it a point to associate with people whose mental attitudes inspire you with enthusiasm, self-confidence, determination, and ambition. Remember that every word spoken within your hearing, every sight that reaches your eyes, and every sense impression that you receive through any of the five senses, influences your thoughts.

This being true, can you not see the importance of controlling, as much as possible, the environment in which you live and work? Can you not see the importance of reading books which deal with subjects that are directly related to your definite chief aim? Can you not see the importance of talking with people who are in sympathy with your aims and who will encourage you and spur you on toward their attainment?

WHATEVER YOU CAN CONCEIVE AND BELIEVE, YOU CAN ACHIEVE

[The following is from **Law of Success**, *Volume I, Lesson Two.]*

Suppose your definite chief aim is far above your present station in life. What of it? It is your privilege—in fact it is your duty—to aim high in life. You owe it to yourself, and to the community in which you live, to set a high standard for yourself.

There is solid evidence that nothing within reason is beyond the possibility of attainment by the person whose definite chief aim has been well-developed.

Some years ago, Louis Victor Eytinge was given a life sentence in the Arizona penitentiary. At the time of his imprisonment he was an all-around "bad man," by his own admissions. In addition to this it was believed that he would die of tuberculosis within a year.

Eytinge had reason to feel discouraged, if anyone ever had. Public feeling against him was intense and he did not have a single friend in the world who came forth and offered him encouragement or help.

Then something happened in his own mind that gave him back his health, put the dreaded disease to rout, and finally unlocked the prison gates and gave him his freedom. What was that "something"?

It was that he had made up his mind to regain his health. It was a very definite chief aim. In less than a year from the time his decision was made, he had won.

Then he extended that definite chief aim by making up his mind to gain his freedom. Soon the prison walls melted from around him.

EDITOR'S NOTE

In prison, Louis Eytinge decided to become a writer. He took magazines, catalogs, and anything else that contained marketing copy, and he began to rewrite it. As his confidence in what he was doing grew, he sent the revised copy to the companies that had produced it. Some were not flattered but others recognized that he had skill. Soon he was earning a good sum of money. But more important, his dedication impressed a group of his clients and they decided to help him. They petitioned the governor of Arizona for clemency. It took some time, but Eytinge was eventually freed and walked out of the prison and into a job with a public relations firm.

The following is adapted from a story told in both **Believe and Achieve** *and in* **The Success System That Never Fails***.*

Napoleon Hill and W. Clement Stone were holding a series of "Science of Success" three-evening seminars in San Juan, Puerto Rico. On the second evening of the course, as homework for the following day, they encouraged participants to apply the principles they had learned and report the results back to the group.

The next night an accountant who was taking the course gave this report:

"This morning when I arrived at work, my general manager, who is also attending this seminar, called me into his office and said, 'Let's see if this really works. You know, we have that $3,000 collection that is months overdue. Why don't you make the collection? Call on the manager, and when you do, use a positive mental attitude. Let's begin with Mr. Stone's self-starter: *Do it now!*'

"I was so impressed by your discussion last night, about how everyone can make their subconscious mind work for them, that when my manager sent me out to make the collection, I decided to try to make a sale also.

"When I left my office, I went home. In the quiet of my home I decided exactly what I was going to do. I prayed sincerely and expectantly for help to make the collection and a large sale.

"I believed I would get specific results. And I did. I collected the $3,000 and made another sale of over $4,000. As I was leaving my customer's office, he said, 'You certainly surprise me. When you came here, I had no intention of buying. I didn't know you were a salesman. I thought you were the head accountant.' That was the first sale I had ever made in my business career."

EDITOR'S NOTE

Throughout his career, Napoleon Hill heard thousands of stories from people who had first approached his theories with some doubt and then were amazed at the results when they actually tried it for themselves. In one of Hill's recorded lectures he quoted a letter he'd received from Edward P. Chase shortly after **Think and Grow Rich** *was published. Chase was a salesman representing Sun Life Assurance, and this is what he said:*

"I am writing to express my grateful appreciation of your book. I followed its advice to the letter. As a result, I received an idea which resulted in the sale of a two-million-dollar life insurance policy, the largest single sale of its kind ever made in Des Moines."

The key to the sale was that Ed Chase did not merely read the book; he "followed its advice to the letter." He wasn't cynical, he didn't question the unusual ideas, he just did what it said, and it delivered exactly what it promised. The moment you set a definite purpose and go after it with a burning desire to achieve, opportunities you did not expect will be placed in your way.

Hill also told about meeting an Australian, Bill McCall, who, as a young man, had been a failure in business until he borrowed a copy of **Think and Grow Rich** *from his local library in Sydney. Bill McCall told Napoleon Hill he distinctly remembered that he was on his third reading of the book, at the chapter on autosuggestion, when it all suddenly came together and clicked in his mind.*

Recognizing his definite chief aim, and fixing it in his character by using the autosuggestion techniques advised in the book, was the turning point for Bill McCall. He claims that without that revelation he would never have become chairman of the board of Coca Cola in Australia, a director of more than twenty family-owned corporations, and the youngest man ever elected a member of the Australian parliament.

Another great example happened closer to home, at radio station WGN in Chicago.

Earl Nightingale, whose radio program "Our Changing World" was heard daily on hundreds of stations, was also a well-known public lecturer, cofounder of one of the first audiobook companies, and the voice of many motivational programs. Because of his interest in self-help material, he read **Think and Grow Rich,** *was fascinated by the chapter on Definite Chief Aim, and decided to test it out. This is what he said in a letter to W. Clement Stone and Napoleon Hill:*

"In over twenty years spent searching for a formula with which a person could utilize every possible element in his favor, it was not until I read Napoleon Hill that I found all the answers.

"Using Dr. Hill's formula for achievement, I was able to double my income in one week. This was quite a feat, because my income previous to this time was rather considerable. I then figured that if it would work once, I could double it again and at the same time remove all doubts as to the efficacy of the procedure. I repeated the process.

"Any person who carefully studies and diligently practices Dr. Hill's proved methods cannot fail to achieve that which he has set his heart on.

"Dr. Hill's work changed my life, and I wholeheartedly recommend it to anyone who is interested in a better life."

It is hard to imagine that Hill's methods could get a better endorsement than having Earl Nightingale personally confirm that the **Think and Grow Rich** *methods had worked for him. But it got even better. Nightingale was so sincere in his praise of the impact Hill's methods had on his life that he took it upon himself to promote Napoleon Hill's book on his radio program for a week without charge.*

CONCENTRATION AND YOUR DEFINITE CHIEF AIM

[The following combines material from How to Sell Your Way Through Life *with a similar material from* Law of Success *and* Think and Grow Rich: The 21st-Century Edition.]*

Nearly everyone has a definite chief aim at one time or another. Ninety-five per cent of the people who have such aims, however, make no attempt to realize them, because they have not learned how to concentrate on their definite aims long enough to fix the aims in their subconscious mind. The majority of people who adopt a definite aim do so more as a wish than in the form of a definite, determined, well-defined intention.

Merely permitting a definite aim to come into your mind won't do you any good. To be of value, your definite aim must be fixed in your mind through the principle of concentration.

The principle behind a definite chief aim and the principle of concentration are two sides of the same coin. One can be applied successfully only with the aid of the other.

The doers are the believers in all walks of life. Those who believe that they can achieve the object of their definite chief aim do not recognize the word *impossible*. Neither do they acknowledge a temporary defeat. They know they are going to succeed, and if one plan fails they quickly replace it with another plan.

Every noteworthy achievement met with some sort of temporary setback before success came. Edison conducted more than ten thousand experiments before he succeeded in making the first talking machine record the words "Mary had a little lamb."

Concentration develops the power of persistence and enables you to master all forms of temporary defeat. Most people never learn the real difference between temporary defeat and permanent failure, because they lack the persistence necessary to stage a comeback after they have experienced temporary defeat. Persistence is merely concentrated effort well-mixed with determination and faith in yourself.

Remember what was taught in the chapter on autosuggestion. You are applying the principle of autosuggestion for the purpose of giving orders to your subconscious mind.

Remember also, unemotional words do not influence the subconscious mind. You will get no appreciable results until you learn to reach your subconscious mind with thoughts or spoken words that have been well emotionalized with belief.

The orders must be presented over and over again (repeated positive affirmation) before they are interpreted by the subconscious mind.

Do not become discouraged if you cannot control and direct your emotions the first time you try.

Your ability to use the principle of autosuggestion will depend, very largely, on your capacity to concentrate on a given desire until that desire becomes a burning obsession.

Make up your mind what you desire, decide to get just that with no substitutes, and you will have taken possession of the most priceless of all assets available to human beings.

But your desire must be no mere wish or hope. It must be a burning desire which is so obsessive that you are willing to pay whatever price its attainment may cost.

The moment you choose a definite major purpose in this way, strange and wondrous things begin to happen. The ways and means of attaining that purpose will begin immediately to reveal themselves to you. The cooperation of others will become available. Your fears and doubts will begin to disappear and self-reliance will take their place.

You now have within your possession the key to achievement. You have but to unlock the door to the temple of knowledge and walk in. But *you* must go to the temple; it will not come to you. If these laws are new to you, the going will not be easy at first. You will stumble many times. Read and reread the chapter on autosuggestion until you understand and have mastered the techniques of visualization and affirmation.

Chapter 5

THE MASTER MIND

EDITOR'S NOTE

When Napoleon Hill wrote the original manuscript of his masterwork **Law of Success,** *the book was constructed around fifteen individual concepts which he called the principles of success. Despite the fact that the book was a runaway bestseller, and that Hill had spent twenty years researching, testing, and writing the material for the book, he still had reservations about some of the content. Hill had come to the realization that a concept he wrote about in the introductory chapter was in fact a principle unto itself. As a result, the next published edition included a new, sixteenth principle of success which Napoleon Hill called the Master Mind. He defined the Master Mind as "coordination of knowledge and effort, in a spirit of harmony, between two or more people, for the attainment of a definite purpose."*

After reading Hill's definition of the Master Mind, many people make the mistaken assumption that what he is describing is nothing more than teamwork. That is not correct. The following explanation should help you understand the difference between teamwork or cooperation (which is certainly desirable and something you should strive for in any endeavor) and a Master Mind alliance, which takes the concept and steps it up to another level. This explanation is adapted from the Napoleon Hill Foundation's book **Believe and Achieve.**

Teamwork can be achieved by any group—even one whose members have disparate interests—because all it requires is cooperation. In teamwork, people might simply be cooperating because they like the leader, or out of a sense of duty. Some team members will give 100 percent to any team that pays them enough, but they have little concern about the objective. And sometimes there is good teamwork *because* different members have different agendas. A board of directors may disagree, even be unfriendly, and still run a business successfully. Musical groups are made up of notoriously self-centered people who work as a team if it will help them get ahead.

Master Minds, on the other hand, are formed of individuals who have the same agenda, a deep sense of mission, and commitment to the same goal. Master Minds represent the highest order of thinking by a group of knowledgeable people, each contributing their absolute best according to their own abilities, expertise, and background. If you have ever been a part of a meeting when everything just clicked and ideas built upon other ideas, with each member contributing until out of the group activity came the best possible idea or solution, that was a Master Mind at work.

POWER THROUGH THE MASTER MIND

[The following section is excerpted and adapted from **Law of Success,** *Volume I, Lesson Two.]*

No individual may have great power without utilizing the Master Mind. Power in great quantities can be accumulated only through the coordinated efforts of more than one mind. No matter how intelligent or well-informed you may be, no one individual, functioning independently, can ever possess great power. The reason is that power must be applied before it is effective. Individuals are limited as to the amount of power they can transmit or apply.

You will have to get others to cooperate with you if you are going to organize your knowledge so that you can turn your plans into power. Organized effort is produced through the coordination of effort of two or more people, who work toward a definite end, in a spirit of harmony.

Andrew Carnegie first brought to my attention the Master Mind principle. Nearly twenty years ago I interviewed Mr. Carnegie for the purpose of writing a story about him. During the interview I asked him to what he attributed his success. With a twinkle in his eyes he said: "Young man, before I answer your question, will you please define your term *success*?"

After waiting until he saw that I was somewhat embarrassed by this request, he continued: "By success you make reference to my money, do you not?"

I assured him that *money* was the term by which most people measured success, and he then said: "Oh, well, if you wish to know how I got my money—if that is what you call success—I will answer your question by saying that we have a Master Mind here in our business, and that mind is made up of more than a score of men who constitute my personal staff of superintendents and managers and accountants and chemists. No one person in this group is the Master Mind of which I speak, but the sum total of all the minds in the group, coordinated, organized, and directed to a definite end in a spirit of harmonious cooperation, is the power that got my money for me. No two minds in the group are exactly alike, but each man in the group does the thing that he is supposed to do and he does it better than any other person in the world could do it."

Carnegie's group of men constituted a Master Mind and that mind was so well-organized, so well-coordinated, so powerful, that it could have accumulated millions of dollars for Mr. Carnegie in practically any sort of endeavor of a commercial or industrial nature. The steel business in which that mind was engaged was but an incident in connection with the accumulation of the Carnegie wealth. The same wealth could have been accumulated had the Master Mind been directed in the coal business or the banking business or the grocery business, because behind that mind was power—that sort of power which you may attain when you have organized the faculties of your own mind and allied yourself with other well-organized minds for the attainment of a specific goal.

EDITOR'S NOTE

There are at least three distinctly different advantages you gain by working with a Master Mind alliance.

First, it increases the amount you can do. As Hill wrote at the beginning of this chapter, no matter how intelligent or well-informed you may be, no one salesperson, functioning independently, can ever possess great power. You need other people to extend your reach. If you try to do it on your own it will take you longer to do things that others can do faster and better; in the end you will waste time, money, and energy.

Second, it improves the quality of what you can do, because in addition to more manpower it also gives you more knowledge than any single person can have. A Master Mind has been called networking of the highest order. Through your Master Mind alliance you combine your advice and knowledge with the advice and knowledge of others who join with you, and the others give you the use of their counsel and contacts just as if it was your own.

Third, it improves your creativity. When the minds of two or more people are coordinated in a spirit of harmony, the energy of each mind seems to pick up on the energy of the other minds. A Master Mind produces that feeling you get when everyone is very focused on the same goal and it is going so well that you seem to be in tune with each other. When that happens, your own work and ideas seem to be operating on a higher and better plane than usual.

The following resumes the original text from **How to Sell Your Way Through Life.**

HOW TO MULTIPLY YOUR BRAINPOWER

The human brain may be compared to an electric battery. It is a fact that a group of batteries will provide more energy than a single battery. It is also a fact that the amount of energy provided by each individual battery depends upon the number and capacity of the cells it contains.

The brain functions in a similar fashion. Some brains are more efficient than others. A group of brains coordinated (or connected) in a spirit of harmony will provide more thought-energy than a single brain, just as a group of electric batteries will provide more energy than a single battery.

When a group of individual minds are coordinated and function in harmony, the increased energy created through that alliance becomes available to every individual mind in the group.

Henry Ford began his business career under the handicap of poverty, illiteracy, and ignorance. Within the inconceivably short period of ten years Mr. Ford mastered these three handicaps, and within twenty-five years he made himself one of the richest men in America.

How did he do it? Here is an important clue: Mr. Ford's most rapid strides became noticeable from the time he became a personal friend of the famed inventor Thomas A. Edison. It is a fact that Mr. Ford's outstanding achievements became even more pronounced later, after he formed the acquaintances of Harvey Firestone, John Burroughs, and Luther Burbank (each a man of great mental capacity).

Through his association with Edison, Burbank, Burroughs, and Firestone, Mr. Ford added to his own brainpower the intelligence, experience, knowledge, and spiritual forces of these four men. Ford used the Master Mind principle in exactly the way it is described in this book.

EDITOR'S NOTE

The first step in putting together your Master Mind alliance is to clearly know your desire or definite chief purpose. Your desire will tell you what you need. It could be a small group, just two or three people, as was the case with Steven Jobs and Steve Wozniak when they formed Apple; Bill Gates and Paul Allen launching Microsoft; or Steven Spielberg, Jeffrey Katzenberg and David Geffen creating DreamWorks SKG. Or it could be a large group, such as the Master Mind alliance of thirty regional directors of Century 21 Real Estate, which founder Arthur Bartlett firmly believes was essential to the company's success. Napoleon Hill suggests that in most cases it should be a dozen people or less, and generally the smaller the better.

Choosing the people means finding those who not only share your vision but who will also share their ideas, information, and contacts with you. They will let you use the full strength of their experience, training, and knowledge as if it were your own. And they will do it in a spirit of perfect harmony.

The question that immediately comes to every reader's mind is, "Where do I find people who will help me to that degree?" Hill cannot answer that question for you, but he does tell you what to look for. Where you look is up to you. And if you really do have the desire to succeed, you will start looking and you won't give up until you find the right people.

Napoleon Hill's description of the Master Mind that appears below includes material from **Think and Grow Rich** *and* **Law of Success,** *and is augmented with additional material from articles and speeches Hill wrote that were compiled for publication by Hill's friend, mentor, and business associate, W. Clement Stone, and appear in two books,* **Napoleon Hill's Keys to Success** *and* **Believe and Achieve.**

FINDING YOUR MASTER MIND MEMBERS

Ally yourself with a group of as many people as you may need in order to assemble a Master Mind that will assist you in creating and carrying out your plan or plans for the accumulation of money. Compliance with this instruction is absolutely essential.

Choose to associate with people who share common values, goals, and interests, yet who each have a strong desire to contribute to the overall effort. Trial and error will be part of the process, but there are two qualities to keep foremost in your mind.

The first is ability to do the job. Do not select people for your alliance merely because you know them and like them. Such people are valuable to you because they improve the quality of your life, but they are not necessarily suited to a Master Mind alliance. Your best friend may not be the most knowledgeable marketing professional, but perhaps he or she can introduce you to someone who is.

The second quality is the ability to work in a spirit of harmony with others. There must be a complete meeting of minds, without any reservations. Personal ambition must be subordinate to the achievement of the purpose of the alliance. This includes your own.

You must also insist upon confidentiality. Some people can give away an idea simply because they love to talk. You don't need them in your group.

Attune yourself to every member of the group. Try to imagine how you would react in a given situation if you were in his or her shoes.

Pay attention to body language. Sometimes facial expressions and movements say far more about what a person feels than the words that come out of his or her mouth.

Be sensitive to what is not being said. Sometimes what is left out is far more important than what is included.

Don't try to force the group along too quickly. Allow for those who want to test ideas by playing devil's advocate.

COMPENSATING YOUR MASTER MIND

Before forming your Master Mind alliance, decide what advantages and benefits you may offer the individual members of your group in return for their cooperation. No one will work indefinitely without some form of compensation. And no intelligent person should request or expect another to work without adequate compensation.

Wealth will obviously have the most appeal to your members. Be fair and generous in your offer.

Recognition and self-expression may be just as important as money to some of your members.

Remember that in such partnerships the principle of going the extra mile (doing more and better than paid for) is especially important. As the leader you should set an example for the others to follow.

Each member must agree at the outset on the contribution each will make, and on the division of benefits and profits. Otherwise, be assured that dissention will arise, you will have wasted everyone's time, you will ruin friendships, and your venture will be destroyed.

MEETING WITH YOUR MASTER MIND

Arrange to meet with the members of your Master Mind group at least twice a week, and more often if possible, until you have jointly perfected the necessary plan or plans for the accumulation of money.

The first meeting will be involved in sorting out strengths and weaknesses, and in fine-tuning your plans. Your alliance must be active to do any good. Establish specific responsibilities and action steps to be taken.

As your Master Mind matures and harmony grows among the members, you will find that the meetings create a flow of ideas into every member's mind. Don't let the meetings become so regular and formalized that they inhibit phone calls and other less formal contact.

MASTER MIND MAINTENANCE

Maintain perfect harmony between yourself and every member of your Master Mind group. If you fail to carry out this instruction to the letter, you may expect to meet with failure. The Master Mind principle cannot work where perfect harmony does not prevail.

Create a nonthreatening environment. Explore all ideas with equal interest and concern for the originator's feelings.

Everyone must deal with everyone else on a completely ethical basis. No member should seek unfair advantage at the expense of others.

As the leader, you must inspire confidence in your members by your dedication to your desire—which is the object of the group. The members must know with certainty that you are reliable, trustworthy, and loyal.

When you are finally ready to present the results of your efforts to investors, buyers, or the public, you may face your greatest leadership challenge in maintaining the harmony of your Master Mind. The group's efforts will now be judged by outsiders, and facing judgment takes courage and persistence.

The courage of separate individuals is nothing compared with that of a united team. The more you are able to maintain harmony, the greater the power. And the greater the power, the more resistance you can overcome.

THE MASTER MIND AND CHANGE

Don't ignore the fact that your chief aim may change and you may have to change your Master Mind associates.

From time to time it may become necessary to change the plans that you have adopted for the achievement of your definite chief aim. Make these changes without hesitation. No one has sufficient foresight to build plans that need no alteration or change.

If any member of your friendly alliance loses faith in the Master Mind, immediately remove that member and replace him or her with some other person.

Andrew Carnegie said to me that he, too, had found it necessary to replace some of the members of his Master Mind. In fact, he said that practically every member of whom his alliance was originally comprised had, in time, been removed and replaced with some other person who could adapt himself more loyally and enthusiastically to the spirit and objective of the alliance.

You cannot succeed when surrounded by disloyal and unfriendly associates, no matter what the object of your definite chief aim may be. Success is built upon loyalty, faith, sincerity, cooperation, and the other positive forces essential to your environment.

Many of you will want to form friendly alliances with those with whom you are associated professionally or in business, with the object of achieving success in your business or profession. In such cases the same rules of procedure which have been described here should be followed. The object of your definite chief aim may be one that will benefit you individually, or it may be one that will benefit the business or profession with which you are connected.

The law of the Master Mind will work the same in either case. If you fail, either temporarily or permanently, in the application of this law, it will be because some member of your alliance did not enter into the spirit of the alliance with faith, loyalty, and sincerity of purpose.

MARRIAGE AND THE MASTER MIND

A Master Mind alliance with the person you love most deeply is of untold importance. If you are married and have not built your relationship on the same principles of harmony that are crucial to any alliance, you may have some reselling to do with your spouse. Set aside time each day to talk about what you want to achieve and how you are going about it. Rely on your definiteness of purpose to build your persuasive abilities to convince your partner of the benefits of the work you are doing. It is very unlikely that your work will not affect your husband or wife in some significant way, and you absolutely must not drag your partner unwillingly into any adventure.

Build your Master Mind alliance into your marriage from the start and it will steady and support you through the darkest moments. In fact, your whole family should be incorporated into your alliance. Lack of harmony at home can easily spill over elsewhere. A united family is a great team.

THE MASTER MIND AND INFINITE INTELLIGENCE

You will recall that in chapter 3 on autosuggestion, the term *infinite intelligence* was used to describe the part of our subconscious where bits and pieces of information come together to create flashes of insight, leaps of logic, and original ideas. Infinite intelligence is also the part of the thinking process which produces hunches, premonitions, and that sensation we refer to as déjà vu. Infinite intelligence also comes into play in a Master Mind alliance.

The human mind is a form of energy. When the minds of two people are coordinated in a spirit of harmony, the energy of each mind seems to pick up on the energy of the other mind. Two heads are not only better than one, they are better than two—because the combination is more than the sum of its parts. No two minds ever come together without creating this third invisible, intangible force, which, in the case of a Master Mind, will produce insights and ideas that neither of the individual minds would have come up with independently.

EDITOR'S NOTE

This chapter would not be complete without including the story of the greatest Master Mind of Napoleon Hill's career, the alliance between Hill and millionaire businessman and philanthropist, W. Clement Stone. This story is also a perfect example of what an enormous impact Napoleon Hill's sales techniques can have on a company's sales force.

The following section is adapted from **A Lifetime of Riches: The Biography of Napoleon Hill,** *with minor excerpts from* **Think and Grow Rich: The 21st-Century Edition** *and* **Believe and Achieve.** *It begins with some background on W. Clement Stone.*

Like Napoleon Hill, W. Clement Stone was born into poverty. Fatherless since the age of three, by the time he was six Stone was peddling papers on the street corners of Chicago's tough South Side to help his mother pay the rent. At thirteen, he owned his own newsstand. At sixteen, his mother pawned her rings so they could move to Detroit where she could become an insurance agent. During the summers, Clem went to work for his mother selling insurance door-to-door. Four years later, W. Clement Stone had managed to scrape and save $100 which he used to move back to Chicago and start his own insurance agency.

From his years selling newspapers, and the lessons learned cold-calling insurance prospects, W. Clement Stone had turned himself into a consummate salesman and motivator. In the beginning, his new Chicago agency did very well. Then came the Depression, and his business was devastated.

In 1937, W. Clement Stone received a copy of Napoleon Hill's hot-selling book *Think and Grow Rich* as a gift from Morris Pickus, a sales consultant who was trying to get Stone to purchase his services. Stone was not much of a prospect for anything that cost money at that time. When *Think and Grow Rich* was placed on his desk, Stone had pared his sales force down to a skeletal group of 135 and was still nearly thirty thousand dollars in debt.

Although Stone had never heard of Hill or his famous bestseller before, the title piqued his curiosity and he opened it up. As he flipped through the pages, Stone became more and more interested in what Hill had to say and finally read the book from cover to cover. He found that Hill's philosophy was very similar to his own and that the book gave him new insights that he could apply to his own business. One of those insights was the Master Mind principle—people working in harmony toward a common goal.

"I had had some concern over hiring men in my office," Stone explained later. "I thought that perhaps some might later become my competitors. The Master Mind principle made me realize that I could multiply my efforts by employing others—individuals of good character—to do much of the work that I was doing or couldn't take the time to do."

Stone was so enthusiastic about the book's blend of inspiration and practical advice that he provided copies of it to every one of his salesmen. "Fantastic things began to happen," he recalled. "Many of my salesmen became supersalesmen. Sales and profits increased. Their attitudes had changed from negative to positive. Those who were searching for the secret of success realized that they had unlimited potential powers to affect their subconscious minds through the conscious.

By 1939, because of the impact that *Think and Grow Rich* had on him personally and on his salesmen, Stone's sales force had swelled to more than one thousand, his company had soared beyond even its pre-Depression peak, and Stone himself was blazing a trail of success that would ultimately rival the likes of Carnegie and Edison.

Jump forward twelve years to 1951. Napoleon Hill was in his sixty-seventh year when he made a conscious decision to reduce his workload. It had been a half century since he left Wise County for the first time in search of fame and fortune. And although he had found both, it had been a fast and wild ride.

On May 2, 1951, Napoleon Hill and his wife Annie Lou drew up a one-page statement of their "immediate major purposes." The signed document focused on income strategies for Nap's semiretirement years. One point called for income from sales of Hill's *Law of Success* home-study textbooks, and two others dealt with the marketing of *Believe and You Shall Achieve*, a manuscript Hill was working on at the time. Another item dealt with collection of a debt from an associate in Rio de Janeiro, and yet another focused on finding sponsors for a television program based on the seventeen principles of success. Few people would associate such an ambitious set of short-term goals with retirement, but Napoleon did.

But even as Napoleon settled back to enjoy his twilight years, fate was spinning yet another web for him. Weeks after drafting and signing his retirement statement, he would fulfill an earlier agreement to speak before a dental convention in Chicago . . . and by fulfilling this obligation, his life and the lives of countless others would be forever changed.

Shortly before Hill's engagement in Chicago, Dr. Herb Gustafson, a Chicago-based dentist who had recommended Hill as a speaker, picked up the phone to repay a favor to one of his favorite patients and finest friends.

The man he was calling had introduced him to Napoleon Hill's work some years earlier by giving him a copy of *Think and Grow Rich.* Dr. Gustafson's friend was something of a philosopher himself and had seized on *Think and Grow Rich* as a great work when it first came out. In fact, Dr. Gustafson's friend had personally purchased several thousand copies of the book over the years, distributing them to his employees and friends.

Gustafson's call was quickly put through and the high voltage voice of W. Clement Stone came on the line with a friendly greeting. "Clem," said Gustafson, "how would you like to hear Napoleon Hill speak next week?"

Stone chuckled. Since Hill had dropped out of the national spotlight some years before, Stone assumed the author-philosopher had died. "Herb," he replied, "I don't think my time has come yet."

The two friends laughed, then Gustafson delivered his news. Not only was Hill still living, he would be appearing in Chicago the following week at a luncheon where Stone was also speaking. At last he could meet the man who had sold him so many books.

Stone himself had achieved fame as a self-made entrepreneur who had amassed a personal fortune and created a dynamic, far-flung company from selling one-dollar travel insurance policies. When word reached Hill that Stone would attend the luncheon, the sixty-seven-year-old semi-retired business evangelist felt a surge of adrenaline. This, Hill thought, could be very interesting.

That sentiment turned out to be one of the rare understatements in Napoleon Hill's long and full life.

Napoleon Hill's adrenaline was still pumping full force when the meeting broke for lunch following his speech.

He had been a smashing success. His highly educated, well-to-do audience had been as captivated and energized by his evangelistic blend of motivational and philosophical messages as any other group he had addressed over the previous fifty years. And while he had enthralled thousands of audiences in his lifetime, the thrill of the experence never eroded. If anything, at age sixty-seven, with his career in the half-speed of semiretirement, the satisfaction from a spine-tingling performance was even greater.

As the cluster of well-wishers and admirers gradually receded and the conventioneers began taking their seats for lunch, W. Clement Stone made his entrance.

Stone was not yet the sort of public figure whose appearance in a crowded room would stop conversations and turn heads. Although he had blazed a wide swath of recognition and respect in the insurance industry, he had no use for publicity and press coverage. He was dedicated to building his business, not a public image, so he tried to stay out of the public limelight. Still, he was a distinctive presence, even to those who didn't know him. Smartly dressed in his trademark dark suit, starched white shirt, and traditional bow tie, Stone radiated energy and self-assurance as he began working the crowd. Not even a Chicago politician was his equal when it came to pressing the flesh with a room full of strangers. He was, after all, the millionaire master of cold-call selling—a man who had amassed a personal fortune selling one-dollar insurance policies without an appointment to people he'd never met before in his life. Nor was he daunted by anyone's station in life. His classic sales strategy was to target a large business—banks were best—and start with the president or the chairman, if the latter were on the premises. After selling the top executive, Stone would work his way down the pecking order to the clerks and maintenance people, pointing out to each prospect that the prospect's boss and the president of the prospect's organization had purchased the same policy.

That strategy, combined with Stone's carefully honed formula for handling the sales situation, had made him an immensely successful salesman; his ability to train others to employ the same strategy and sales tactics had led to the creation of his own army of supersalespeople and a personal fortune for Stone.

Stone's interest in *Think and Grow Rich*, and in Hill himself, stemmed directly from his belief that there were formulas one could follow to achieve success in sales, in a career, and in life. The canvassing strategies he employed were one kind of formula; the "scripts" he created for his salespeople and himself to use in the selling situation were another kind of formula. But Stone knew that a truly successful salesperson needed more than a script and a basic strategy. He or she also needed a philosophical formula that would help them shake off the despair of a bad day or week, overcome the contentedness that could follow a great week, and resolve the inevitable conflicts between career and family, ambition and principles, and the many other doubts and dichotomies that can erode one's performance.

Hill's principles of success were a near perfect adjunct to Stone's own selling formulas and disciplines. Indeed, from the time he read *Think and Grow Rich* in 1938, there were two absolutes in Stone's business: Every new salesperson he hired was trained in his formula, many by Stone himself, and each of the thousands of salespeople in his organization got a copy of *Think and Grow Rich* from Stone . . . and was required to read it.

True to his word, Herb Gustafson ushered Stone to the speaker's table and sat him next to Hill. As Gustafson completed the introductions, Stone enthusiastically told Hill that he was one of his biggest customers, having purchased thousands of copies of *Think and Grow Rich* for his salespeople over the past decade. He also told Hill that the book had been instrumental in his rise to great wealth.

Hill beamed with delight. Praise was something he always valued from any source. Praise from accomplished men and women was even more stimulating. But this was more than praise. It was an endorsment of his life's work, and it came from a man who was more than accomplished. Stone was, in Hill's eyes, an empire builder cut from the same mold as the giants of early twentieth-century American industry whose philosophies had provided the basis for Hill's principles of success.

Hill's quiet semiretirement fell into jeopardy as Stone finished his brief greeting. After nearly a half century of trials and tribulations, Hill's mission from Carnegie had come full circle. He had assembled, analyzed, and popularized the qualities that bred the greatest figures in American business history, and he had lived to meet a man whose modern greatness was linked through Hill's own work to those of Carnegie's generation. Suddenly, Hill was only aware of how much more could be done.

W. Clement Stone was on the same wavelength. A lifelong goal-setter, by 1952, he had two primary goals. His business goal was to build his thirty-million-dollar empire to the one-hundred-million-dollar level. His personal goal was to use his wealth and knowledge to "create a better world for this and future generations." Stone would later refer to this altruistic resolve as his "magnificent obsession," after reading Lloyd C. Douglas's *The Magnificent Obsession.* The connection between Stone's goals and Hill's rejuvenated sense of activism became clear to both men as the luncheon progressed.

"If you want to know someone," Stone taught his salespeople, "get them to talk about themselves." Stone applied his own teachings to his first meeting with Hill. He broke the ice by asking questions about Hill's speech. He quickly found it didn't take much to get Napoleon Hill started. Even at age sixty-seven, Hill spoke with an unrelenting intensity and animation that kept even a veteran listener like Stone on the edge of his seat. Soon, Stone's questions were no longer inspired by polite curiosity. He began probing the depths of a man whose energy, ideas, and captivating delivery could have a tremendous impact on his business and his humanitarian goals.

By the end of the luncheon, Hill and Stone had carved the foundation for a Master Mind alliance. They had debated Hill's belief that the

most important principle of success was a definite major purpose—
Stone believed a positive mental attitude came first—and they had
shared anecdotes and philosophies on a wide range of subjects. As the
creative sparks flew, Stone turned on his most persuasive selling charm
and told Hill he should forget about retirement and come back to a
world that needed him as much as it ever had.

Hill countered with the wisdom gained from a half century of
accomplishment and failure: He would do just that, but only if Stone
himself would manage his activities. Hill had learned all too well that
there was more to a great message than a great delivery; to be really
successful needed organization, pragmatic planning, and powerful
backing. W. Clement Stone could offer all these qualities and more
—and he did.

In the speeches and writings of his lifetime, Napoleon Hill offered
dozens, perhaps hundreds of different examples of Master Mind alliances,
but none would ever achieve the scope, depth, longevity, and impact
of the alliance that he and Stone forged over the ensuing months and
decades. They would never have a contract; their working agreement
would always be based on common goals, and their business relationship
was based on trust and a handshake.

In August 1952, after Napoleon completed the remainder of his
public-appearance obligations, Stone put Hill on his payroll and their
partnership began in earnest with the formation of Napoleon Hill
Associates. Still living in California, Napoleon plunged into the creation
of a new book as well as the new home-study textbooks that he and
Stone had decided were central to their project. He also commuted
regularly to Chicago to help Stone design and implement a new training
program for Stone's salespeople.

Stone's previous approach to sales training focused on new employees:
He or one of his sales managers would take new salespeople out on

calls, show them how to apply the strategy and scripts, then stay with the initiate long enough to ensure that he or she had mastered the process. Following that introduction, salesmanship was reinforced mainly through Stone's daily sales letters, which were a mixture of motivational messages, and reviews of basic selling principles.

Despite the legendary success of his sales force, Stone believed that the performance of even his best salespeople could be dramatically improved if they received periodic face-to-face retraining and reinforcement. He also believed that this was the key to Combined's continued growth.

Stone's new training program called for assembling groups of salespeople for several days at a time to review the company's basic sales strategies and tactics, to drill them on new and old formulas for handling a wide variety of sales situations, and, most of all, to rejuvenate their enthusiasm.

The availability of Napoleon Hill to work in this program was a rich blessing, and Stone knew it. Not only could Hill brew great froths of inspiration anywhere people gathered, but his message and his philosophy would stay with them even after the echoes of his spoken words faded to silence and their world became once again a place where failure lurked along the trail to each day's opportunities.

Many of Stone's salespeople had outspoken doubts about this new program, despite the boss's enthusiastic promotion of it. They were concerned about losing time in the field, and, most of all, they could conceive no earthly benefit from a discourse on the philosophy of success by a man whose book on the subject they had already read.

But that came before they experienced the program. Afterward, it was a different story. Literally hundreds of Combined Insurance Company salespeople found themselves operating at new performance levels as they applied both the latest "blueprints" for selling created by Stone and Hill's time-tested principles of success for meeting the challenges of life and career.

Despite his gift for hyperbole in describing his own accomplishments, not even Napoleon Hill could embellish on his actual contribution to the remarkable ensuing growth of Stone's empire. Combined Insurance Company's sales increased at a dizzying pace, and Stone used the profits to expand into disability and life insurance by acquiring more companies, which themselves enjoyed tremendous growth.

"I really hit the jackpot with Napoleon Hill," Stone remarked many years later. "Motivation was the key to growing from where we were, and nobody could motivate people like Napoleon Hill."

But the profitability and growth of Combined Insurance Company of America was only a by-product of the Stone-Hill Master Mind alliance. Their definite main purpose was to improve their own society by communicating the principles of success to millions of people of all walks of life, of all races and religions. The organization they established to accomplish all this was based on altruistic goals, but it was not a charity.

Within a year they had launched Napoleon Hill Associates; they published new books by Hill including *How to Raise Your Own Salary* and *The Master Key to Riches*; they reissued Hill's earlier bestsellers; they co-authored a new bestseller, *Success Through a Positive Mental Attitude*. They also launched *Success Unlimited* magazine, created the Science of Success home-study courses, made television programs, radio shows, a documentary film—*A New Sound in Paris*, which showed the amazing change that happened when the entire town of Paris, Missouri, adopted the Napoleon Hill philosophy—and they both criss-crossed America speaking, teaching, giving interviews, and spreading the philosophy to as many people as possible.

EDITOR'S NOTE

During the years of Hill's active participation, Stone's $30 million company grew to reach $100,000,000 in assets. When W. Clement Stone passed away in 2002, his company, now known as AON Corporation, had revenues of $2 billion a year, and W. Clement Stone had personally given more than $275 million to various charitable and philanthropic organizations. Stone would trace much of his company's success to the man he lured out of retirement in 1952.

There has perhaps never been a greater example of "coordination of knowledge and effort, in a spirit of harmony, between two or more people for the attainment of a definite purpose." The sheer volume of work and scope of influence achieved in a ten-year period by Napoleon Hill and W. Clement Stone leaves little question as to the power and importance of a Master Mind alliance.

Chapter 6

PERSONALITY & CHARACTER

EDITOR'S NOTE

The opening segment of this chapter is adapted from **Law of Success,** *Volume III, Lesson Ten, with additional material from* **How to Sell Your Way Through Life.**

No one can have a pleasing personality without the foundation of a sound, positive character. You may wear the best and latest clothes, and conduct yourself in a most pleasing manner outwardly, but in some way you telegraph the nature of your character to those with whom you come in contact. There is a great power of attraction in the person who has a positive character, and this power expresses itself in unseen as well as visible ways. The moment you come within speaking distance of such a person, even though not a word is spoken, the influence of the unseen power within makes itself felt.

Acquire the habit of making yourself agreeable and you profit both materially and emotionally, for you will never be as happy in any other way as you will be when you know that you are making others happy.

If there is greed and envy and hatred and jealousy and selfishness in your heart, you will never attract anyone except those who are the same. Like attracts like, and you may be sure that those who are attracted to you are those whose inward natures parallel your own.

You may present an artificial smile and you may practice handshaking so that you can imitate, perfectly, the handshake of a person who is adept at this art, but if these outward manifestations of a pleasing personality lack that vital factor called earnestness of purpose, they will turn people away rather than attract them to you.

Every shady transaction in which you engage, every negative thought that you think, and every destructive act destroys something within your character.

The big prizes of life go to the builders and not to the destroyers. The man who builds a house is an artist; the man who tears it down is a junkman.

SELLING IS AN ART

[The following resumes from **How to Sell Your Way Through Life.***]*

The act of selling, when done by a master, may be compared to an artist at an easel. Stroke by stroke, just as an artist develops form and harmony and blends the colors on a canvas, the master salesperson paints a word-picture of the thing being offered for sale. The canvas is the imagination of the prospective buyer. The artist first roughly outlines the picture, later filling in the details, using ideas for paint. In the center of the picture, at the focal point, is drawn a clearly defined outline of motive. Just as a painting on a canvas must be based upon a theme or a motive, so must a successful sale.

The picture that the master sales artist paints in the mind of the prospective buyer must be more than a mere skeleton outline. Details must be perfected so the prospect not only sees the picture in perspective as a finished whole, but the picture must be pleasing. Motive is the thing that determines how pleasing the picture can be made.

Amateurs and little children may draw a rough picture of a horse that can be recognized to be the picture of a horse. But when the master artist draws a picture of a horse, those who see it not only recognize it as a horse, but they also exclaim, "How wonderful! It is like it is alive!" The artist paints action, reality, and life into the picture.

The inefficient salesperson hurriedly sketches a crude outline of the thing he or she wishes to sell, leaving motive out of the picture. That kind of salesperson says, "See, there it is, as plain as the nose on your face. Now will you buy?" But the prospective buyer does not see what the salesperson has kept hidden within their own mind. Or the buyer may "see" but does not feel. The buyer is not moved to action by any rough sketch or unfinished, lifeless picture. No seed of desire has been planted in the buyer's mind; no appeal to motive.

The master salesperson paints another picture. The master omits no detail. He or she mixes word-colorings so that they blend with harmony and symmetry that capture the prospective buyer's imagination. The master salesperson builds the picture around a motive which dominates the entire scene, putting the prospective buyer's own mind to work. That is master salesmanship.

A little while ago a salesman came to sell me life insurance. As everyone knows, life insurance is an abstract; intangible and one of the hardest things in the world to sell. You cannot see it; you cannot smell it, taste it, feel it, or sense it through any of the five senses. In addition, you must die in order to profit by it. Even then, the profit goes to someone else.

But this salesman was a thorough professional. Through study and preparation, he had familiarized himself with the motives that most quickly and effectively appeal to the majority of prospective purchasers of life insurance. He had prepared himself to analyze his prospective buyers accurately in order to figure out which motive was best suited to each case.

His sales presentation was almost as if he had placed before me an invisible canvas, and on this canvas, with only words for brushes, he caused me to see an image of myself as I will be when my hair is graying, my shoulders are stooped, my hand trembles, and my walk falters.

I do not mean that he actually described that scene, but through a hint dropped here and a well-chosen word mentioned there, I could not help but see that vision in my mind.

And what about my dependents? He played that loaded word *dependent* like a master violinist playing upon the strings of a Stradivarius. What about my wife whose future I would surely want to make secure?

Even though she is still a young woman of vigor, beauty, and independence, I was soon getting flashes of myself cold in my coffin, and my wife, now frail, aging, and left without means or future security.

It takes a real sales artist to paint such a vivid word-picture. Master salesmanship consists of a series of picture impressions imprinted on the mind of the prospective buyer through one or more of the five senses. If these word-pictures are not clear and distinct, beautifully harmonized, and properly seeded with motive, they will not move the prospective buyer to action.

Master salespeople paint pictures in the minds of their prospective buyers through as many motives and through as many of the senses as possible. When they can, they supplement the word-pictures with real pictures and samples. They know that sales are more easily made when the presentation reaches the mind of the prospective buyer through more than one of the five senses and when more than one motive for buying has been planted in the buyer's mind.

Master salesmanship begins and ends with proper motive. As long as the right motive has been injected into the selling argument, it makes very little difference what happens between the opening and closing of a sale.

All selling is like this. People are moved to buy or not to buy because of motive. Base your sales presentation upon the right motive and your sale is made before you start.

Dr. Harper, who sold the streetcar magnate on endowing the building at the university, was not a born salesperson. He was small in physique and unprepossessing in appearance. He became a great salesperson by studying people and the motives that cause them to act. That is exactly what you must do if you want to become a master at sales. You must study people and you must understand motivation.

Just as with artists who work in oils, even though you may be born with talent you only become a finished artist by studying and mastering technique. Sales artists, too, are made and not born. They become masters by studying technique and motive; they develop expert methods of analyzing buyers and the things they buy.

SHOWMANSHIP

People buy personalities and ideas much more quickly than they buy merchandise. For this very reason the salesperson who is a good showman makes sales where other salespeople cannot. A good showman is one who can dramatize the commonplace events of life and give them the interesting appearance of uniqueness. Showmanship calls for sufficient imagination to be able to recognize things, people, and circumstances that are capable of being dramatized.

The life insurance salesperson who is a showman and possesses a magnetic personality sells everything except statistics, and seldom mentions the word *policy*. He or she does not have to. They deal in ideas and use them to paint alluring pictures that interest and please the prospective buyers.

A good showman makes effective use of enthusiasm. The poor showman knows nothing of enthusiasm, instead trusting to colorless statements of fact and appeals to the prospective buyer's reason. Most people are not influenced by reason; they are swayed by emotion. The salesperson who is not capable of arousing his or her *own* emotions is not going to appeal to others through their emotional nature.

A sales presentation delivered by a person with showmanship is a show all by itself and as interesting as a play or a movie. It carries the prospective buyer through exactly the same mental processes that a good drama does.

A salesperson who is an able showman can change the prospective buyer's mind from negative to positive. The master salesperson accomplishes this change of mental attitude not by accident or luck, but by a carefully prearranged plan. Regardless of the state of mind the buyer may be in when approached, an able showman "neutralizes" the mind of the prospective buyer. And what is more important, the able showman knows enough not to try to close the sale until this change has been successfully effected.

If you are a gardener you cannot grow plants without preparation of the soil before the seed is sown. If you are a salesperson you can't plant the seed of desire in the prospective buyer's mind while that mind is negative. The salesperson who understands showmanship prepares the mind of the prospective buyer as carefully and scientifically as the intelligent gardener prepares the ground.

William Burnette took an ordinary sales plan, added showmanship, and turned it into a multimillion-dollar income in less than five years. The basic sales plan itself was quite straight forward and, at that time, not at all uncommon: create a sales force to sell aluminum cookware to housewives.

The average order-taker salesperson might tell you that the entire plan can be described in one sentence: Burnette is going to get his salespeople to organize clubs of housewives for the purpose of selling them aluminum cookware.

A master with a flare for showmanship like Burnette would tell you his plan is to give all the hardworking housewives in the neighborhood a break by throwing a lunch party in their honor. And the best part is that he will do the catering and show them how to make cooking a breeze.

How William Burnette's sales plan actually worked was as follows: He would select a nice middle-class neighborhood and make an arrangement to use the home of a local woman who would invite all of her friends and neighbors to a lunch party. All of the expenses would be paid by Burnette's company, there would be gifts and prizes, an elaborate meal would be prepared by Burnette or one of his salespeople in a flashy demonstration of the aluminum ware he was selling, and the hostess would also earn a commission on the orders taken.

When you examine this sales plan, it quickly becomes apparent that it is much more creative than simply "organizing clubs of housewives for the purpose of selling them aluminum cookware." First, Burnette had developed some very solid sales strategies:

1. Using a local neighborhood hostess was a big help in qualifying and neutralizing the potential buyers.

2. The party atmosphere and the chance to get something for nothing further neutralized the buyers.

3. Having the salesperson do the cooking and serving ensured that the products were shown off to their best advantage.

4. The lunch party allowed Burnette to get all the neighbors in one place so he could present the product to many buyers all at the same time.

By now most readers will have recognized that William Burnette's sales plan became the model for many successful companies that sell everything from kitchenware to cleaning products, cosmetics, and even lingerie. And if you've ever attended one of these sales parties you will also know that it takes showmanship to pull it off. As good a sales plan as it is, if the person running things doesn't have a showman's personality, the event will fall flat and sales will be even flatter.

TAKE AN INTEREST IN OTHERS

[The following is adapted from material in **Law of Success**, *Volume III, Lesson Ten.]*

There is one way that your personality will always attract, and this is by taking an honest interest in other people. Let me illustrate exactly what I mean, by relating an incident that taught me a lesson in master salesmanship.

One day an elderly lady called at my office and sent in her card with a message saying that she must see me personally. No amount of coaxing by secretaries could induce her to disclose the nature of her visit. I assumed that she was some poor old soul who wanted to sell me a book.

As I walked down the hallway from my private office, this lady, who was standing just outside of the railing that led to the main reception room, began to smile. I had seen many people smile, but never before had I seen one who smiled so sweetly as did this lady.

It was one of those contagious smiles, because I caught the spirit of it and began to smile too. As I reached the railing, the lady extended her hand to shake hands with me. Now, as a rule, I do not become too friendly when a person calls at my office, because it is very hard to say no if the caller should ask me to do something that I do not wish to do.

However, this lady looked so innocent and harmless that I extended my hand. I discovered that she not only had an attractive smile but she also had a magnetic handshake. She took hold of my hand firmly, but not too firmly, and made me feel that she was really and truly glad to shake my hand. And I believe that she was.

I have shaken hands with many thousands of people during my public career, but I do not recall ever shaking hands with anyone who understood the art as well as this lady did. The moment she touched my hand I could feel myself "slipping" and I knew that whatever it was she had come after, she would go away with it.

At a single stroke, this lady had cut through that false shell into which I crawl when salespeople come around. This gentle visitor had "neutralized" my mind and made me want to listen.

Slowly and deliberately, as if she had all the time in the world (which she did have, as far as I was concerned at that moment), she began to crystallize the first step of her victory into reality by saying, "I just came here to tell you that I think you are doing the most wonderful work of any man in the world today."

Every word was emphasized by a gentle, but firm, squeeze of my hand, and she was looking through my eyes and into my heart as she spoke. I reached down, unlocked the secret latch that fastened the gate, and said, "Come right in, dear lady—come right into my private office."

For three-quarters of an hour I listened to one of the most brilliant and charming conversations I have ever heard, and my visitor was doing all the conversing.

Was she trying to sell me a book? No. However, she was selling me something, and that something was myself. She had no sooner been seated than she unrolled a package, and sure enough, there was a book in it. In fact, several of them. But what she had was a complete year's file of the magazine of which I was then editor, *Hill's Golden Rule*. She turned the pages of those magazines and read places that she had marked here and there, assuring me in the meanwhile that she had always believed the philosophy behind what she was reading.

Then, after I was in a state of complete mesmerism and thoroughly receptive, my visitor tactfully switched the conversation. During the last three minutes of her visit, she skillfully laid before me the merits of some securities she was selling. She did not ask me to purchase, but the way in which she told me about the securities had the psychological effect of making me want to purchase. And even though I made no purchase of securities from her, she made a sale—because I picked up the telephone and introduced her to a man to whom she later sold more than five times the amount that she had intended selling me.

If that same woman, or another woman, or a man, who had the tact and pleasing personality that she had, should call on me, I would again sit down and listen for three-quarters of an hour.

We are all human, and we are all more or less vain. And we will listen with intense interest to those who talk to us about that which lies closest to our hearts. But that is not the end of the story.

A few years later, in the city of Chicago, I was conducting a sales course for an investment house which employed more than fifteen hundred salespeople. To keep the ranks of that big organization filled, we had to train and employ six hundred new salespeople every week. Of the thousands of men and women who went through that school, there was but one man who grasped the significance of the principle I have just described.

This man had never tried to sell securities, and frankly admitted when he entered the class that he was not a salesman. After he had finished his training, one of the "star" salesmen, a man by the name of Perkins, took a notion to play a practical joke on him. This star gave him an inside "tip" as to where he would be able to sell some securities without any great effort. Perkins would make the sale himself, he said, but the man to whom he referred as being a likely purchaser was an ordinary artist who would purchase with so little urging that he, being a star, did not wish to waste time on him.

The new salesman was delighted to receive the tip and went quickly on his way to make the sale. As soon as he was out of the office, the star gathered together the other "stars" and told of the joke he was playing, for in reality the artist was a very wealthy man and Perkins had spent nearly a month trying to sell to him, without success. It then came out that all the "stars" of that particular group had also called on this same artist but had failed to interest him.

The new salesman was gone about an hour and a half. When he returned he found the stars waiting for him with smiles on their faces.

To their surprise, this new salesman also wore a broad smile on his face. They looked at each other inquiringly.

"Well, did you sell to your man?" asked the originator of the joke.

"Certainly," replied the uninitiated one, "and I also found that artist to be all you said he was—a perfect gentleman and a decidedly interesting man."

Reaching into his pocket he pulled out an order and a check. The stars wanted to know how he did it.

"Oh, it wasn't difficult," replied the new salesman. "I just walked in and talked to him a few minutes, then he brought up the subject of the securities himself and said he wanted to purchase. Therefore, I really did not sell to him. He purchased of his own accord."

When I heard of the transaction, I called this new salesman in and asked him to describe, in detail, just how he made the sale.

He said that when he reached the artist's studio he found him at work on a picture. So engaged in his work was the artist that he did not see the salesman enter, so the salesman walked over to where he could see the picture and stood there looking at it without saying a word. When the artist finally saw him, the salesman apologized for the intrusion and began to talk—about the picture the artist was painting.

He knew just enough about art to be able to discuss the merits of the picture with some intelligence, and he was really interested in the subject. He liked the picture and frankly told the artist so.

For nearly an hour those two men talked of nothing but art, particularly the picture that stood on the artist's easel. Finally, the artist asked the salesman his name and his business, and the salesman replied, "Oh, never mind my business or my name. I am more interested in you and your art."

The artist beamed. But not to be outdone by his polite visitor, he insisted on knowing what mission had brought him to his studio.

Then, with an air of genuine reluctance, this salesman—this real star—introduced himself and told his business. Briefly he described the securities he was selling, and the artist listened as if he enjoyed every word that was spoken.

After the salesman had finished, the artist said, "Well, well! Other salesmen from your firm have been here trying to sell me some of those securities, but they talked of nothing but business. In fact they annoyed me so that I had to ask one of them to leave; I believe his name was Perkins. But you present the matter so differently."

And how did this new salesman present the matter so differently? What did this master salesman really sell that artist? Did he sell him securities?

No! He sold him his own picture that he was painting on his own canvas. The securities were almost incidental.

It happens that in a class attended by this new salesman early on, I had told the story of the elderly lady who entertained me for three-quarters of an hour by talking about that which was nearest my heart, and it had so impressed him that he made up his mind to study his prospective purchasers and find out what would interest them most, so he could talk about that.

In his first month, this "green" salesman earned in commissions more than double what the next-highest salesman earned. And the tragedy of it was that not one person out of the entire organization of fifteen hundred salespeople took the time to find out how and why he became the real star of the organization.

EDITOR'S NOTE

Because there is a tendency to read examples like the two preceding stories and assume "that was then, but this is now," where possible, the editors make a point of including contemporary stories that make the same point. As you will see in the following example adapted from the Napoleon Hill Foundation's book **Believe and Achieve,** *the technique Hill wrote about is still being studied and written about by modern business theorists.*

In their book *Modern Persuasion Strategies: The Hidden Advantage in Selling*, Donald J. Moine and John H. Herd refer to "pacing," by which they mean revealing your own personality traits that are similar to those exhibited by a person you are trying to influence. Pacing, they say, is "a sophisticated form of matching or mirroring key aspects of another's behavioral preferences."

What Donald Moine and John Herd suggest is not a contrived sort of cozying-up that most of us automatically find distasteful, but rather a genuine form of identifying with another and stepping into stride with that person.

Some people do it naturally while others have to work at it, but the net result is the same. "You are pacing," the authors say, "when the prospect gets the feeling that you and he (or she) think alike and look at problems in similar ways. When this happens, the prospect identifies with you and finds it easy and natural to agree with you. You seem like emotional twins. Pacing works, because like attracts like."

Another reason pacing works is that selling, like most other people relationships, is emotional. People don't buy your products, your ideas, or fund your projects on reason alone. They respond emotionally to a well-thought-out, logical, persuasive, *emotional* appeal. Regardless of the degree of sophistication of today's prospects, Moine and Herd believe, selling is still more emotional than objective.

In the course of doing research for their book, the authors studied one hundred of the country's top sales producers who say they "cannot consciously describe how they perform their own sales magic." After studying them in action, reviewing their tapes, and testing the newfound insights in the field, Moine and Herd realized that these supersales-people so naturally identified with people that prospects instantly liked them, and bought their products and services. Teaching others these pacing techniques resulted in sales increases in some companies of as much as 232 percent in the span of one year.

While it is possible to pace yourself to align the compatible aspects of your personality with another's, this is not to suggest that you should become a chameleon mimicking others.

Emphasize those aspects of your personality that you like in yourself and that others find attractive. Because we are all complex individuals with a full range of positive and negative emotions, it would be totally unrealistic to expect everyone you meet to like every aspect of your personality. But, by directing your thoughts, you can control the kind of person you wish to become; a positive thinker becomes a positive person, someone others like to be around.

When you are dealing with others, look for a common ground. Identify the subjects you are both interested in, not just those *you* like or are particularly knowledgeable about. When you are having a conversation with someone else, don't just take turns talking, *listen* to what the other person is saying.

To borrow another technique from the sales field, allow the other person to talk by asking probing, open-ended questions. Supersalesman Hank Trisler says in his book *No Bull Selling,* "A salesman should talk twenty percent of the time and listen eighty percent of the time, and that twenty percent ought to be questions to get the customer talking more. The quickest way to establish rapport is to get the other guy talking about himself. The more you let me talk about myself, the better I like you," he says.

RECAP OF ELEMENTS OF A PLEASING PERSONALITY

[The following resumes from **How to Sell Your Way Through Life.***]*

The elements of a pleasing personality are:

I. *Good showmanship.* A showman is someone who appeals to people through their imagination and keeps them interested through curiosity. A good showman is quick to recognize and to capitalize on other people's likes and dislikes at the psychological moment.

2. *Harmony with yourself.* You cannot have a pleasing personality without first developing harmony and control in your own mind.

3. *Definiteness of purpose.* The procrastinator who drifts through life without a plan or purpose does not have a very pleasing personality.

4. *Appropriateness of style and clothing.* First impressions are lasting. Inappropriate clothing style creates an impression that is difficult to overcome. The person with a pleasing personality dresses in clothing appropriate to the situation.

5. *Posture and carriage of the body.* Everyone judges others by their body language: the way they walk and the general posture of their bodies. Alertness in physical attitude indicates an alert mind and keenness of perception.

6. *Voice.* The tone, volume, pitch, and general emotional coloring of the voice constitute important factors of a pleasing personality.

7. *Sincerity of purpose.* This quality needs little explanation, but having it is essential if you want to earn the confidence of others.

8. *Choice of language.* The person with a pleasing personality is comfortable talking in the common vernacular or speaking formally. And, just as important, the person with a pleasing personality knows which to use when.

9. *Poise.* Poise is a quality that comes naturally to a person with self-confidence and self-control.

10. *A good sense of humor.* Perhaps no other quality is more essential than this.

11. *Unselfishness.* Selfishness and a pleasing personality are never found together.

12. *Facial expression.* Facial expression is an accurate medium for the interpretation of your moods and thoughts. You can have a big smile, a crooked grin, or it may be as subtle as a twinkle in the eye, but you can always tell if it is sincere.

13. *Positive thought.* The vibrations of your thoughts are picked up by others. To be pleasing, you must be radiating good feelings and pleasant thoughts.

14. *Enthusiasm.* People who lack enthusiasm cannot inspire others. Enthusiasm is an essential factor in all forms of salesmanship.

15. *A sound body.* Poor health does not attract people. You cannot be enthusiastic without health and vigor.

16. *Imagination.* Imagination is one of the most essential factors of a pleasing personality.

17. *Tact.* Lack of this quality has cost many people their positions. Lack of tact is usually expressed through insensitivity to others and through loose conversation.

18. *Versatility.* General knowledge of the important subjects of current interest, and the deeper problems of life and living, is a quality conducive to a pleasing personality.

19. *The art of being a good listener.* Train yourself to listen attentively when other people are speaking.

20. *The art of forceful speech.* Forceful speech is the salesperson's greatest asset. It is an art that can only be acquired by practice. Have something to say that is worth listening to, then say it with all the enthusiasm at your command.

21. *Personal magnetism.* This is also called charisma, and it is the major asset of every great salesperson and every great leader in all walks of life. It is this factor of a pleasing personality that is the hardest to teach. Each person has some charisma to some degree. You must discover your own charismatic quality, then make the most of what you have.

A sales manager, who has trained more than thirty thousand salespeople, came to the conclusion that individuals who are most confident sexually are the most efficient salespeople. The explanation is that the personality factor known as charisma is a manifestation of sexual energy.

EDITOR'S NOTE

The following comments on charisma and salesmanship are from Hill's bestselling masterwork, **Think and Grow Rich: The 21st-Century Edition:**

There have been numerous psychological and sociological studies about the relationship between sexuality and success that tend to support Hill's observation. Because physical characteristics are the most quantifiable aspects of sexuality, most research studies focus on gender, attractiveness, body size, and age, and they measure indicators such as first impressions, expectation of performance, perception of performance, and social interaction.

The studies generally conclude that when comparing individuals of equal competence, for men the perception is that taller men will do better than short, a full head of hair will outperform balding, and handsome or virile will beat out plain or older. For women the results are comparable. The perception is that attractive performs better than plain, slim or shapely scores higher than overweight, and younger is expected to be superior to older.

These observations about physical sexuality may seem obvious, but they lead to a conclusion that is very significant. Obviously not all people who succeed are tall and virile or attractive and shapely. It is also a fact that the success of those who are short, balding, plump, or plain isn't always due to superior skill or luck. Clearly there is another kind of attractiveness that often supersedes physical appeal.

This other kind of attractiveness is connected to human sexuality, but it is not what would usually be referred to as "sexy." People who have this quality are often said to have "chemistry," "personality," "charm," "appeal"—or "charisma."

When employing salespeople, a good sales manager looks for charisma as the first requirement. People who lack this kind of sexual energy will never become enthusiastic nor inspire others with enthusiasm. And enthusiasm is one of the most important requisites in salesmanship, no matter what you are selling.

The public speaker, preacher, lawyer, or salesperson who is lacking in charisma is a flop, as far as being able to influence others is concerned. That, plus the fact that most people are influenced through an appeal to their emotions, should easily convince you of the importance of charisma as a part of the salesperson's ability. Master salespeople attain mastery in selling because they either consciously or unconsciously transmute charisma (sexual energy) into sales enthusiasm.

That statement explains the actual, practical meaning of sexual transmutation.

The meaning of the word *transmute* is, in simple language, "the changing, or transferring, of one element or form of energy into another." The transmutation of sexual energy means switching the mind from thoughts of physical expression, to thoughts of some other nature.

Salespeople who know how to turn on charisma have acquired the art of sexual transmutation, whether they know it or not. The majority of salespeople who transmute their sexual energy do so without being aware of what they are doing, or how they are doing it.

You can cultivate and develop this quality in your dealings with others. Through cultivation and understanding, this vital motivating force may be drawn upon and used to great advantage in relationships between people. This energy may be communicated to others in the following ways:

- *The vibrations of thought.* People with charisma project sexuality through their personality in a way that influences those around them.

- *Clothing and style.* People who are charismatic are usually very careful about their personal appearance. They usually select clothing of a style becoming to their personality, physique, complexion, and so on.

- *The handshake.* The touch of the hand indicates, instantly, the presence of charisma or the lack of it.

- *Posture and carriage of the body.* People with charisma move briskly, and with grace and ease.

- *The tone of voice.* Charisma, or sexual energy, is the factor with which the voice may be colored or made musical and charming.

[This is the end of the comments on charisma excerpted from **Think and Grow Rich: The 21st-Century Edition.** *We resume from* **How to Sell Your Way Through Life.***]*

ELEMENTS OF A NEGATIVE PERSONALITY

We come now to the qualities that constitute a negative personality. Analyze and check yourself carefully.

1. *Disloyalty.* There is no substitute for loyalty! The person who lacks loyalty cannot possibly market personal services effectively.

2. *Dishonesty.* There is no substitute for honesty! It is the keystone to character. Without sound character, no person can market their services effectively.

3. *Greed.* A person who is cursed by greed cannot keep it under cover.

4. *Envy and hatred.* These qualities make having a pleasing personality impossible. Like attracts like.

5. *Jealousy.* This is a mild form of insanity. It is fatal to a pleasing personality.

6. *Anger.* Whether passive or active in form, this is a quality that arouses antagonism and makes one disliked by others.

7. *Fear.* There are six basic fears against which every person must guard. These are negative states of mind that must be eliminated before one may develop a pleasing personality.

8. *Revenge.* A vengeful person cannot be pleasing to anyone.

9. *Fault finding.* The person who has the habit of finding fault with others might more profitably spend time looking within for their own faults.

10. *Gossiping about scandal.* People may listen to the scandal-monger, but they will not like the person.

11. *Uncontrolled enthusiasm.* Too much enthusiasm is as bad as none.

12. *Excuses.* It is better to take responsibility for mistakes you do not make than to form the habit of trying to place responsibility for these mistakes on others.

13. *Exaggeration.* It is better to understate a truth than to overstate it. Exaggeration causes loss of confidence.

14. *Egotism.* Self-confidence is one of the most desirable and necessary traits, but it must be controlled and directed to definite ends. All forms of self-praise are easily recognized as evidences of inferiority complexes. Therefore, your motto should be "Deeds, not words."

15. *Obstinacy and stubbornness.* A certain amount of determination and the ability to stand by your opinions is essential, but these qualities should not become a blanket policy.

16. *Selfishness.* No one likes a selfish person. This quality attracts opposition in every conceivable form.

Remember, when you step before the mirror of your own conscience, that this book was written as a means of helping people to market their services effectively by first understanding and improving what they have to market. Keep this thought clearly in mind and be your most severe critic as you read. Developing a pleasing personality is up to you. It calls for self-control and a willingness to change destructive habits.

THE GOLDEN RULE

[The following segment is excerpted and adapted from **Law of Success,** *Volume IV, Lesson Sixteen.]*

There are people who believe that the Golden Rule—"Do unto others as you would have them do unto you"—is nothing more than a theory and is in no way connected with an actual law of nature. They have arrived at this conclusion because of personal experience wherein they rendered service to others without getting something in return.

How many of us have not rendered service to others that was neither reciprocated nor appreciated? I have had such an experience many times and I am equally sure that it will happen again in the future. But I will not discontinue rendering service to others merely because they neither reciprocate nor appreciate my efforts. And here is the reason: When I render service to another, or indulge in an act of kindness, I store away in my subconscious mind the effect of my efforts. By doing so, I will become a certain kind of person, and because I am that kind of person I will attract to me other people who harmonize with or resemble my own character. And those whom I attract to me will be the kind who will reciprocate acts of kindness and service. Thus, what I call the law of compensation will have balanced the scales for me. I do believe that this is indeed a natural law that influences our lives.

Because of this great truth it is impossible for you to render any useful service or indulge in any act of kindness toward others without benefiting from it. Moreover, it is just as impossible for you to indulge in any destructive act or thought without paying the penalty in the loss of a corresponding degree of your own power.

In effect, "do unto others as you would have them do unto you" and "an eye for an eye and a tooth for a tooth" are two sides of the same coin. One is the positive and the other is the negative. Even the most selfish person will respond to this double-edged sword. They cannot help it. If I speak ill of you, even though I tell the truth, you will not think kindly of me. Furthermore, you will most likely retaliate in kind. But if I speak of your virtues, you will think positively of me and, in the majority of instances, when there is an opportunity you will also reciprocate in kind.

Perhaps it should be "do unto others as you would have them do unto you—bearing in mind that human nature has a tendency to retal-iate in kind." In other words, if you would rather not have your own eye plucked out, then ensure against this misfortune by refraining from plucking out the other fellow's eye. Furthermore, render the other fellow an act of kindly helpful service, and through the operation of this same law he will render you a similar service.

And if he should fail to reciprocate your kindness, what then?

You will have profited nevertheless—because of the effect of your act on your own subconscious mind.

Thus, by indulging in acts of kindness and always applying the Golden Rule philosophy, you are sure of benefit from one source and at the same time you have a pretty fair chance of profiting from another source.

It is possible that you could base all your acts toward others on the Golden Rule without ever getting anything back. In the meantime, however, you have been strengthening your own character and sooner or later this positive character you have been building will begin to assert itself and you will discover that you have been receiving compound interest for those acts of kindness that appeared to have been wasted on those who neither appreciated nor reciprocated them.

One reason for being just toward others is that such action may cause them to reciprocate in kind, but as I have said, a better reason is that kindness and justice toward others develops positive character in all who do so.

You may withhold from me the reward to which I am entitled for rendering you helpful service, but no one can deprive me of the benefit I will derive from the rendering of that service insofar as it adds to my own character.

EDITOR'S NOTE

The following segment is excerpted and adapted from **Law of Success,** *Volume III, Lesson Ten.*

Here is a Golden Rule exercise that is guaranteed to improve your character and your personality. Find at least one person each day in whom you see some good quality that is worthy of praise—and praise them for it. Remember that this praise must not be in the nature of cheap, insincere flattery; it must be genuine. Speak your words of praise with such earnestness that they will impress those to whom you speak.

Then watch what happens. You will have rendered those whom you praise a benefit of great value to them, and you will have gone just one more step in the direction of developing the habit of looking for and finding the good qualities in others.

I cannot overemphasize the far-reaching effects of this habit of praising, openly and enthusiastically, the good qualities in others, for this habit will soon reward you with a feeling of self-respect and manifestation of gratitude from others that will modify your entire personality. Here, again, the law of attraction enters, and those whom you praise will see, in you, the qualities that you see in them. Your success in the application of this formula will be in exact proportion to your faith in its soundness.

I do not merely believe that it is sound—I know that it is—and the reason I know is that I have used it successfully and I have also taught others how to use it successfully. Therefore, I have a right to promise you that you can use it with equal success.

Furthermore, you can, with the aid of this formula, develop a pleasing personality so quickly that you will surprise all who know you. The development of such a personality is entirely within your own control, which gives you a tremendous advantage and at the same time places the responsibility on you if you fail or neglect to exercise your privilege.

Chapter 7

ENTHUSIASM & SELF-CONTROL

EDITOR'S NOTE

The following is excerpted from **Law of Success**, *Volume II, Lesson Seven.*

During his administration as sales manager of the National Cash Register Company, Hugh Chalmers (who later became famous in the motor car industry) faced a most embarrassing situation which threatened to wipe out his position as well as that of thousands of salesmen under his direction. The company was in financial difficulty. This fact had become known to the salesmen in the field, and as a result they began to lose their enthusiasm. Sales began to dwindle until finally the conditions became so alarming that a general meeting of the sales organization was called, to be held at the company's plant in Dayton, Ohio. The salesmen were called in from all over the country.

Mr. Chalmers presided over the meeting. He began by calling on several of his best salesmen to tell what was wrong out in the field that orders had fallen off. One by one they got up, as called, and each had a most terrible tale of grief to tell. Business conditions were bad, money was scarce, people were holding off buying until after the presidential election, and so forth. As the fifth man began to enumerate the difficulties that had kept him from making his usual quota of sales, Mr. Chalmers jumped up on top of a table, held up his hands for silence, and said, "Stop! I order this convention to come to a close for ten minutes while I get my shoes shined."

Then turning to a young boy who sat nearby, he ordered the boy to bring his shoeshine kit and shine his shoes, right where he stood, on top of the table.

The salesmen in the audience were astounded! They began to whisper among themselves. Meanwhile, the boy shined first one and then the other shoe, taking plenty of time and doing a first-class job.

After the job was finished, Mr. Chalmers handed the boy a dime, then went ahead with his speech: "I want each of you," he said, "to take a good look at this boy. He has the concession for shoe-shining throughout our plant and offices. His predecessor was considerably older than himself, and despite the fact that the company subsidized him with a salary, that boy could not make a living in this plant, where thousands of people are employed.

"This boy not only makes a good living, without any subsidy from the company, but he is actually saving money out of his earnings each week, working under the same conditions, in the same plant, for the same people.

"Now, I wish to ask you a question: Whose fault was it that the older boy did not get more business? Was it his fault, or the fault of his buyers?"

In a mighty roar from the crowd the answer came back: "It was the boy's fault, of course!"

"Just so," replied Chalmers, "and now I want to tell you this, that you are selling cash registers in the same territory, to the same people, with exactly the same business conditions that existed a year ago, yet you are not producing the business that you were then. Now whose fault is that? Is it yours, or the buyers'?"

Again the answer came back with a roar: "It is our fault, of course!"

"I am glad that you are frank to acknowledge your faults," Chalmers continued, "and I now wish to tell you what your trouble is. You have heard rumors about this company being in financial trouble and that has killed off your enthusiasm so that you are not making the effort that you formerly made. If you will go back into your territories with a definite promise to send in five orders each during the next thirty days, this company will no longer be in financial difficulty, for that additional business will see us clear. Will you do it?"

They said they would, and they did!

That incident has gone down in the history of the National Cash Register Company under the name Hugh Chalmers' Million-Dollar Shoe Shine, for it is said that this turned the tide in the company's affairs and was worth millions of dollars.

Enthusiasm knows no defeat! The sales manager who knows how to send out an army of enthusiastic salespeople may set his or her own price on their services. What is more important even than this, they can increase the earning capacity of every person under their direction. Thus, the sales manager's enthusiasm benefits not only themselves, but perhaps hundreds of others as well.

EDITOR'S NOTE

The remainder of this entire chapter, Enthusiasm & Self-Control, is adapted from **Law of Success,** *Volume II, Lesson Seven and Lesson Eight, with minor additions from* **Think and Grow Rich** *and* **How to Sell Your Way Through Life.** *In those instances where longer passages have been included, the original source is noted.*

WHAT YOU SAY, DO, AND THINK

Anyone who has seen enthusiasm spread to an audience realizes that there is some form of unspoken communication going on. When your mind is working at a high rate because it has been stimulated with enthusiasm, you send out vibrations that register in the minds of all within its radius—and especially in the minds of those with whom you come in close contact.

When a public speaker senses the audience is in harmony with him or her, the speaker is merely recognizing that their own enthusiasm has influenced the minds of the listeners until the listeners' minds are vibrating in harmony with the speaker's own.

Whenever a salesperson senses that the psychological moment for closing a sale has arrived, he or she merely feels the effect of their own enthusiasm as it influences the mind of the prospective buyer and places that mind "en rapport" with the salesperson's own.

As a salesperson, your enthusiasm or your lack of enthusiasm is conveyed to your potential buyers in three ways: what you say, what you do, and what you think.

When you are enthusiastic over the goods you are selling, the services you are offering, or the speech you are delivering, your state of mind becomes obvious to all who hear you, by the tone of your voice.

Whether you have ever thought of it in this way or not, it is the tone in which you make a statement, more than it is the statement itself, that carries conviction or fails to convince. No mere combination of words can ever take the place of a deep belief in a statement that is expressed with burning enthusiasm. Words are just sounds unless they are colored with feeling that comes from enthusiasm.

Here the printed word fails me, for I can never express with mere type and paper the difference between words that fall from unemotional lips, without the fire of enthusiasm behind them, and those that seem to pour forth from a heart that is bursting with eagerness for expression. The difference is there, and it is obvious when you hear it.

Thus, what you say, and the way in which you say it, conveys a meaning that could be just the opposite of what is intended. This accounts for many a failure by salespeople who present arguments in words that seem logical enough but lack the coloring that can come only from enthusiasm that is born of sincerity and belief in the goods they are trying to sell. Their words said one thing, but their tone of voice suggested something entirely different. Therefore, no sale was made.

SPEAK WITH FORCE AND CONVICTION

No matter what your calling in life may be, you should be able to stand on your feet and speak convincingly.

Remember that speech is the chief method of expressing your personality, and for this reason it is to your advantage to cultivate a style that is both forceful and pleasing. You should work on your voice until it becomes rhythmical and pleasing to the ear. If your voice is inclined to be high-pitched, tone it down until it is soft and pleasing. Put feeling and emotion into your words as you speak, and develop a rich tone of voice.

Study the outstanding figures in politics and statesmanship and you will see that the most successful ones are those who are noted for their ability to speak with force and conviction. The same is true in business, industry, and finance. The most prominent leaders are men and women who are able public speakers.

As a salesperson you may never have to deliver a public address, but you will profit anyway because this ability will increase your power to speak convincingly in ordinary conversation.

EDITOR'S NOTE

You must exercise your voice the same way you do your other muscles. If it is going to be strong and reliable, you must work out, you must practice, you must rehearse, and you must test yourself.

The only way for you to really know how your voice sounds to others is to record yourself. You will likely be surprised by how different it sounds when you hear it played back. Analyze the recording to find where and how you could make improvements. Note the tone, the pitch, and the rhythm of your speech patterns. Do your words flow smoothly, or do you stop and start and interrupt yourself with ums and ahs? Just by hearing yourself you will be able to make many improvements.

There are some very good audio programs that will guide you through exercises to improve breathing, tone, and control. Naturally, there are also professional voice coaches. And you should not discount what can be learned by joining organizations such as Toastmasters clubs.

The only way to really know how you look to others is to work in front of a mirror, or better yet, video-record yourself. The impression you make on others depends on how well you project your personality, how passionately you make your points, and how comfortable you look doing it. Record your presentation, play it back, make notes about everything that you want to change, with special attention paid to your facial expressions and your hand gestures. Looking like you don't know what to do with your hands is a sure indicator that you are inexperienced as a speaker.

Just as there are vocal coaches, there are also acting coaches and other professional consultants who can help you improve your physical presentation. Again, the editors encourage you to research your local Toastmasters and other such speaking clubs, drama clubs, or performing classes. Although you can learn much from audio and video programs, or from taking courses, in the end, the more you actually stand up and do it, the better you will be.

Just as important as the sound of your voice and your delivery are the words you use. Unless you are certain of the exact meaning of a word, don't use it. Opt instead for one that is more familiar to you. There are many books available that point out some of the common mistakes people make in an attempt to sound more knowledgeable. One of the best-known is **The Elements of Style** *by William Strunk Jr. and E. B. White, a small but extremely good resource that offers information for both the spoken and written word.*

There are also speech courses available on tape and CD that not only teach new vocabulary but also allow you to hear the words used in context while hearing the correct pronunciation. You will find these audio programs in the audiobook section of most large bookstores.

In **The Success System That Never Fails,** *W. Clement Stone advises that to sound enthusiastic you must act enthusiastic. If you act enthusiastic your emotions will follow and soon enough you will feel enthusiastic. He offers the following specific advice from his own experience:*

1. Talk loudly! This is particularly helpful if you are emotionally upset or if you have "butterflies in your stomach" when you stand before an audience.

2. Talk rapidly! Your mind functions more quickly than you do.

3. Emphasize! Stress words that are important to you or your listeners —a word like *you*, for example.

4. Hesitate! Talk rapidly, but hesitate where there would be a period, comma, or other punctuation mark in the written words. When you employ the dramatic effect of silence, the mind of the person who is listening catches up with the thoughts you have expressed.

5. Hesitation after a word you wish to emphasize accentuates the emphasis.

6. Keep a smile in your voice! This eliminates gruffness as you talk loudly and rapidly. You can put a smile in your voice by putting a smile on your face, a smile in your eyes.

7. Modulate! This is important if you are speaking for a long period. Remember, you can modulate both pitch and volume. You can speak loudly, but intermittently change to a conversational tone and a lower pitch if you wish.

[This is the end of the excerpt from **The Success System That Never Fails.** *The following resumes from* **How to Sell Your Way Through Life.***]*

PRACTICE WHAT YOU PREACH

What you say is of course an important factor in the operation of the principle of suggestion, but perhaps even more important is what you do. Your acts will count for more than your words, and woe unto you if the two fail to harmonize.

If you preach the Golden Rule as a sound rule of conduct, your words will fall upon deaf ears if you do not practice what you preach.

If a salesman for Ford drives up to his prospective purchaser in a Buick, all the arguments he can present on behalf of the Ford will be without effect.

Your thoughts constitute the most important of the three ways in which you convey enthusiasm, because they control the tone of your words and your actions. If your thoughts and your actions and your words harmonize, you are bound to influence others.

When a kind-hearted old gentleman once planted in my mind the suggestion that I was a "bright boy" and that I could make my mark in the world if I would educate myself, it was not so much what he said as it was the enthusiastic way in which he said it that made such a deep and lasting impression on my mind. It was the way in which he gripped my shoulders, and the look of confidence in his eyes, that drove his suggestion so deeply into my subconscious mind that it never gave me any peace until I commenced taking the steps that led to the fulfillment of the suggestion.

This is a point I would stress with all the power at my command. It is not so much what you say as it is the *tone* and the *manner* in which you say it that makes a lasting impression.

It naturally follows, therefore, that sincerity of purpose, honesty, and earnestness must be placed behind all that you say if you want to make a lasting and favorable impression.

Whatever you successfully sell to others, you must first sell to yourself.

DO WHAT YOU LOVE, LOVE WHAT YOU DO

[The following story, excerpted from the Napoleon Hill Foundation's book **Believe and Achieve,** *is a perfect example of what can happen when you are enthusiastic because you are totally sold on your product.]*

Some people are blessed with a natural enthusiasm. Mary Kay Ash, founder of Mary Kay Cosmetics, considers herself such a person. She says that she first discovered she could sell on sheer enthusiasm when she was a young housewife and mother.

One day, she recalls, a woman by the name of Ida Blake came to her door selling *The Child Psychology Bookshelf,* a series of books for children. "If you had a problem with your child," Ash says, "you simply looked up the problem in the back of the book, and there was a story to tie in with it. All the stories included very good morals, and whatever the problem was, there was a story to fit the situation. As a young mother trying to teach her children the difference between right and wrong, I just thought those were the best books I'd ever seen!

"When the saleslady told me what they cost, I almost cried. I just couldn't afford them. Sensing my interest, she let me keep them over the weekend, and I read every page. When she came by to pick them up, I was heartbroken. I told her I was going to save my money, and one day I would buy those books, because they were the best I'd ever seen.

"When she saw how excited I was, she said, 'I'll tell you what, Mary Kay, if you sell ten sets of books for me, I'll give you a set.' Well, that was just wonderful! I started calling my friends and the parents of my beginner Sunday-school students at Tabernacle Baptist Church. I didn't even have any books to show them, I just had my enthusiasm."

In a day and a half, Ash sold the ten sets and Ida Blake signed Mary Kay as a saleswoman. Mary Kay went on to make the line of cosmetics that bears her name a household word, and made millions for herself in the process.

EDITOR'S NOTE

If, unlike Mary Kay, you weren't born with natural enthusiasm, you can still develop enthusiasm. You do it by acting enthusiastic. As was pointed out in the chapters Autosuggestion and A Definite Chief Aim, any action that you repeat often enough will become an automatic reflex. It will become your natural habit.

Your emotions may not always respond to reason, but they do always respond to action. By consistently acting enthusiastic, your emotions *will respond and soon you won't just be acting; you will begin to feel enthusiastic. And when you **feel** enthusiastic, you **are** enthusiastic.*

According to W. Clement Stone, "Having enthusiasm is a positive mental attitude—an internal force of intense emotion. Being enthusiastic is an impelling external expression of action."

When you act enthusiastically, you are using the power of suggestion and autosuggestion. In so doing, the salesperson who regularly and repeatedly acts enthusiastic by speaking to others in an enthusiastic and sincere manner soon finds that he or she has developed genuine enthusiasm.

Although Napoleon Hill advises that you act as though you are enthusiastic, and he encourages you to alter your habits and develop a pleasing personality, he also makes it very clear that there is a big difference between putting your best foot forward and putting on a false front. Honesty, sincerity, integrity, modesty, character—these are all qualities at the heart of Hill's philosophy of personal achievement, as is evident from the following.

YOU CAN'T DECEIVE YOURSELF

*[This section is excerpted and adapted from **Law of Success**, Volume II, Lesson Seven.]*

Not long ago I was approached by an agent of the government of a certain country. The agent sought my services as a writer of press and publicity materials for the administration in charge at that time. His approach was about as follows:

"Whereas, you have a reputation as an exponent of the Golden Rule philosophy, and whereas, you are known throughout the United States as an independent who is not allied with any political faction, would you be gracious enough to come to our country, study the economic and political affairs, then return to the United States and write a series of articles to appear in the newspapers, recommending to the people of America the immediate recognition of the government by the United States," et cetera.

For this service I was offered more money than I thought I would ever possess during my entire life. But I refused the commission. I could not write convincingly of that country's cause because I did not believe in that cause. Therefore, I could not have mixed sufficient enthusiasm with my writing to have made it effective, even if I had been willing to dip my pen into ink that I believed to be muddy.

I do not believe that I can afford to try to deceive anyone, about anything, *but I know that I cannot afford to try to deceive myself.* To do so would destroy the power of my pen and render my words ineffective.

No one can become a master salesperson if they compromise falsehood. If you compromise with your own conscience, it will not be long before you have no conscience; for your conscience will fail to guide you, just as an alarm clock will fail to awaken you if you do not heed it.

There is but one thing in the world that gives us real and enduring power, and that is character. Reputation, bear in mind, is not character. Reputation is that which people are believed to be; character is that which people are.

Character is something that you cannot beg or steal or buy. You can get it only by building it; you can build it by your own thoughts and deeds, and in no other way.

Through the aid of autosuggestion, any person can build a sound character, no matter what their past has been. I wish to emphasize the fact that all who have character have enthusiasm and personality sufficient to attract others who have character.

THE PSYCHOLOGY OF GOOD CLOTHES

Enthusiasm is never a matter of chance. There are certain stimuli that produce enthusiasm, the most important being as follows:

1. Occupation in the work that one loves best.
2. An environment where one comes in contact with others who are enthusiastic and optimistic.
3. Financial success.

4. Complete mastery and application, in one's daily work, of the seventeen laws of success.

5. Good health.

6. Knowledge that one has served others in some helpful manner.

7. Good clothes, appropriate to the needs of one's occupation.

These sources of stimuli are self-explanatory, with the exception of the last one. The psychology of clothes is understood by very few people. Clothes are the most important part of the embellishment that every person must have in order to feel self-reliant, hopeful, and enthusiastic.

EDITOR'S NOTE

Needless to say, clothing and what is acceptable to wear in business today is a far cry from what was considered appropriate in the early part of the twentieth century. As you begin to read the following you may wonder what Napoleon Hill, who wore celluloid collars and spats, could have to say to a world where Casual Friday is common and billion-dollar deals are signed by people dressed in blue jeans or sweats.

The editors assure you that if you read on, it will become abundantly clear that the philosophy behind the words supersedes the fashion of any particular era, and that in fact Hill's psychology of good clothes has a much more significant point than "Can I wear checks with stripes?"

When the good news came that the World War was over, my worldly possessions amounted to little more than they did the day I came into the world.

The war had destroyed my business and made it necessary for me to make a new start.

My wardrobe consisted of three well-worn business suits and two uniforms which I no longer needed.

Knowing all too well that the world develops its first and most lasting impressions of a person by the clothes he or she wears, I lost no time in visiting my tailor. Happily, my tailor had known me for many years, therefore he did not ask when I was going to pay for those expensive suits.

With less than a dollar in change in my pocket, I picked out the cloth for three of the most expensive suits I ever owned, and ordered that they be made up for me at once. One of the suits was a beautiful dark gray; one was a dark blue; the other was a light blue with a pinstripe.

I then purchased three less expensive suits and a complete supply of the best shirts, collars, ties, hosiery, and underwear that he carried.

The following day the first of the three suits was delivered. I put it on at once, stuffed a new silk handkerchief in the outside pocket of my coat, shoved the fifty dollars I had borrowed on my ring down into my pants pocket, and walked down Michigan Avenue in Chicago, feeling as rich as Rockefeller.

Every morning I dressed myself in an entirely new outfit and walked down that same street at precisely the same hour. That hour "happened" to be the time when a certain wealthy publisher usually walked down the same street on his way to lunch. I made it my business to speak to him each day, and occasionally we would stop for a minute's chat.

This daily meeting had been going on for about a week, when he stopped and motioned me over to the edge of the sidewalk, placed his hand on my shoulder, looked me over from head to foot, and said: "You look damned prosperous for a man who has just laid aside a uniform. Who makes your clothes?"

"Well," I said, "Wilkie & Sellery made this particular suit."

He then wanted to know what sort of business I was engaged in. I said, "Oh, I am preparing the copy for a new magazine that I am going to publish."

"A new magazine, eh?" he queried. "And what are you going to call it?"

"It is to be named Hill's Golden Rule."

"Don't forget," said my publisher friend, "that I am in the business of printing and distributing magazines. Perhaps I can serve you also."

That was the moment for which I had been waiting. And I can assure you, that conversation never would have taken place had this publisher observed me walking down that street from day to day with a "whipped-dog" look on my face, an unpressed suit on my back, and a look of poverty in my eyes.

An appearance of prosperity attracts attention always, with no exceptions whatsoever. Moreover, a look of prosperity attracts "favorable attention," because the one dominating desire in every human heart is to be prosperous.

My publisher friend invited me to his club for lunch. Before the coffee and cigars had been served he had "talked me out of" the contract for printing and distributing my magazine. I had even "consented" to permit him to supply the capital, without any interest charge.

For the benefit of those who are not familiar with the publishing business, let me point out that considerable capital is required for launching a new nationally distributed magazine. The capital necessary for launching Hill's Golden Rule Magazine was raised because of the way I was dressed and, perhaps more important, the way the clothes made me feel.

I not only knew that correct clothes would impress others favorably, but I knew also that good clothes would give me an air of self-reliance, without which I could not hope to regain my lost fortunes.

I have met many salespeople in my time. During the past ten years I have personally trained and directed the efforts of more than three thousand men and women, and I have observed that, without a single exception, the star producers were all people who understood and made good use of the psychology of clothes. I have yet to see the first poorly dressed salesperson who became a star producer.

Success attracts success! There is no escape from this fact. Therefore, if you wish to attract success, make sure you look the part of success, whether your calling is that of day laborer or merchant prince.

For the benefit of the more "dignified" students of this philosophy, who may object to resorting to "trick clothing" as a means of achieving success, let me say that the real lesson here is that practically every successful person has discovered some form of stimulus through which they can and do drive themself on to greater effort.

I have often gone into business meetings with colleagues who had the appearance of worry written all over them, only to see those same colleagues straighten up their shoulders, tilt their chins at a higher angle, soften their faces with smiles of confidence, and get down to business with that sort of enthusiasm which knows no defeat.

If a person goes about the affairs of life devoid of enthusiasm, they are doomed to failure. Nothing can save them until they change their attitude and learn how to stimulate their mind to heights of enthusiasm at will.

ENTHUSIASM AND SUGGESTION

We will now analyze the subject of suggestion, and I will show you exactly how to apply the principle upon which it operates. Suggestion differs from autosuggestion in only one way—we use suggestion, consciously or unconsciously, when we influence others, while we use autosuggestion as a means of influencing ourselves.

Before you can influence another person through suggestion, that person's mind must be in a state of neutrality; that is, it must be open and receptive to your method of suggestion. Right here is where most salespeople fail—they try to make a sale before the mind of the prospective buyer has been rendered receptive or neutralized.

When I say that the salesperson must neutralize the mind of the prospective purchaser before a sale can be made, I mean that a state of confidence must have been established. It is obvious that there can be no set rule for either establishing confidence or neutralizing the mind to a state of openness. Here the ingenuity of the salesperson must supply that which cannot be set down as a hard-and-fast rule.

Some years ago I wrote a book entitled *How to Sell Your Services*. Just before the manuscript went to the publisher, I wrote to some celebrities to enquire if they would provide me with endorsements to be published in the book. The printer was waiting for the manuscript, therefore I hurriedly wrote a letter to some eight or ten people, in which I briefly outlined exactly what I wanted.

To my dismay, the letter brought back no replies. I had failed to observe two important prerequisites for success: I had written the letter so hurriedly that I had failed to inject the spirit of enthusiasm into it, and I had neglected to word the letter so that it had the effect of neutralizing the minds of those to whom it was sent. I had not paved the way for the application of the principle of suggestion.

After I realized my mistake, I then wrote a letter that was based on strict application of the principle of suggestion. This letter not only brought back replies from all to whom it was sent, but many of the replies were masterpieces and served, far beyond my fondest hopes, as valuable supplements to the book.

To best show you how the principle of suggestion may be used in writing a letter, and especially what an important part enthusiasm plays in the written word, the two letters are here reproduced. It will not be necessary to indicate which letter failed, as that will be quite obvious:

My dear Mr. Ford:

I am just completing a manuscript for a new book entitled *How to Sell Your Services*. I anticipate the sale of several hundred thousand of these books and I believe those who purchase the book would welcome the opportunity of receiving a message from you as to the best method of marketing one's personal services.

Would you, therefore, be good enough to give me a few minutes of your time by writing a brief message to be published in my book? This will be a big favor to me personally, and I know it would be appreciated by the readers of the book.

Thanking you in advance for any consideration you may care to show me, I am,

Yours very truly . . .

Hon. Thomas R. Marshall,
Vice President of the United States,
Washington, D.C.

My dear Mr. Marshall:

Would you care for the opportunity to send a message of encouragement, and possibly a word of advice, to a few hundred thousand of your fellow men who have failed to make their mark in the world as successfully as you have done?

I have about completed a manuscript for a book to be entitled *How to Sell Your Services*. The main point made in the book is that service rendered is cause and the pay envelope is effect, and that the latter varies in proportion to the efficiency of the former.

The book would be incomplete without some words of advice from a few men who, like yourself, have come up from the bottom to enviable positions in the world. Therefore, if you will write me of your views as to the most essential points to be borne in mind by those who are offering personal services for sale, I will pass your message on through my book, which will ensure its getting into hands where it will do a world of good for a class of earnest people who are struggling to find their places in the world's work.

I know you are a busy man, Mr. Marshall, but please bear in mind that by simply calling in your secretary and dictating a brief letter, you will be sending forth an important message to possibly half a million people. In money this will not be worth to you the two-cent stamp that you will place on the letter, but, if estimated from the viewpoint of the good it may do others who are less fortunate than yourself, it may be worth the difference between success and failure to many a worthy person who will read your message, believe in it, and be guided by it.

Very cordially yours . . .

Let us analyze the two letters and find out why one failed while the other succeeded. This analysis should start with one of the most important fundamentals of salesmanship: motive.

The opening paragraph of the first letter violates an important fundamental of salesmanship, because it suggests that the object of the letter is to gain some advantage for its writer and it does not even hint at any advantage to the person to whom it is sent. Instead of neutralizing the mind of the recipient of the letter, as it should do, it has just the opposite effect: it makes it easy for him to say no.

The reader can clearly see that the object of the letter is to secure an endorsement that will help sell the book, but the benefit to the reader only appears in this sentence: "I believe those who purchase the book would welcome the opportunity of receiving a message from you as to the best method of marketing one's personal services." The most important selling argument—in fact, the only selling argument—has been lost because it was not brought out and established as the real motive for making the request.

Now look at the sentence in the second paragraph that begins, "This will be a big favor to me personally..." The truth is that most people will not grant favors just to please others. If I ask you to render a service that will benefit me, without bringing you some corresponding advantage, you will not be enthusiastic about granting that favor. But if I ask you to render a service that will benefit a third person, and if that service is of such a nature that it is likely to reflect credit on you, the chances are that you will render the service willingly.

However, the most damaging suggestion of all is: "Thanking you in advance for any consideration you may care to show me." This sentence strongly suggests that the writer anticipates a refusal. It clearly indicates a lack of enthusiasm, and there is not one single word in the entire letter that places in the reader's mind a satisfactory reason for complying with the request.

Suggestion is one of the most subtle and powerful principles of psychology. You are making use of it in all that you do and say and think. But unless you understand the difference between negative and positive suggestions, you may be using it in such a way that it is bringing you defeat instead of success.

Let us now review the second letter, which brought replies from all to whom it was sent . . .

> "Would you care for the opportunity to send a message of encouragement, and possibly a word of advice, to a few hundred thousand of your fellow men who have failed to make their mark in the world as successfully as you have done?"

Compare this opening paragraph with that of the first letter. This paragraph is worded as it is for a twofold purpose. First, it is intended to serve the purpose of neutralizing the mind of the reader so he will read the remainder of the letter with an open-minded attitude. And second, it asks a question that can be answered in only one way and at the same time practically forces the reader to accept that object as being sound and reasonable. Any person who would answer the question in the negative would be admitting that he is selfish.

The second paragraph of the letter is a straightforward state-ment of fact that the reader can neither question nor deny. It takes him the second step of the psychological journey that leads straight toward compliance with the request that is carefully clothed in the third paragraph of the letter.

The third paragraph begins by paying the reader a nice little compliment:

> "The book would be incomplete without some words of advice from a few men who, like yourself, have come up from the bottom to enviable positions in the world. Therefore, if you will write me of your views as to the most essential points to be borne in mind by those who are offering personal services for sale, I will pass your message on through my book, which will ensure its getting into hands where it will do a world of good for a class of earnest people who are struggling to find their places in the world's work."

Study the wording, together with the setting in which it has been placed, and it hardly appears to be a request at all. Certainly there is nothing about it to suggest that the writer of the letter is requesting a favor for his personal benefit. At most, it can be construed merely as a request for a favor for others.

Next read the closing paragraph and notice how tactfully concealed is the suggestion that if the reader should refuse the request, he will appear as though he does not care enough about those who are less fortunate than himself to spend a stamp and a few minutes of time for their benefit. This brings the reader up with a bang and turns his own conscience into an ally of the writer.

The best evidence that this analysis is correct is that the letter brought replies from every person to whom it was sent, despite the fact that every one of the recipients was of the type that is generally supposed to be too busy to answer a letter of this nature.

None of them wrote merely to please me, for I was unknown to all but four of them. They wrote to please themselves and to render a worthy service.

SELF-CONTROL

Self-control serves as the balance wheel of enthusiasm. Lack of self-control is the average salesperson's most damaging weakness.

The point I wish to clearly establish in this lesson is that thought, whether accurate or inaccurate, is the most highly organized functioning power of your mind, and that you are but the sum total of your dominating or most prominent thoughts.

If you would be a master salesperson of goods or of your personal services, you must exercise sufficient self-control to shut out all adverse arguments and suggestions. Many salespeople have so little self-control that they hear the prospective purchaser say no, even before it is said. They have so little self-control that they actually suggest to themselves that their prospective purchaser will say no when asked to purchase their wares.

The person with self-control not only makes the self-suggestion that the prospective purchaser will say yes, but if the desired yes is not forthcoming, they stay on the job until the opposition breaks down.

The master salesperson, whether engaged in selling merchandise or personal services or sermons or public addresses, understands how to control their own thoughts. Instead of being a person who accepts, with meek submission, the suggestions of others, the master salesperson is one who persuades others to accept his or her suggestions. The master salesperson becomes a dominating personality.

A master salesperson is one who takes the offensive, and never the defensive, side of an argument if argument arises.

If you are a master salesperson you know that it will be fatal to your sale if you permit the buyer to place you on the defensive and keep you there. You may, and of course you will at times, be placed in a position in which you will have to assume the defensive side of the conversation for a time. But it is your business to exercise such perfect poise and self-control that you will change places with your prospective purchasers without them noticing that you have done so. This requires the most consummate skill and self-control.

Many sweep this vital point aside by becoming angry and trying to scare the prospective purchaser into submission, but the master of the craft remains calm and serene, and usually comes out the winner.

Whenever I use the term *salesperson*, I mean all people who try to persuade or convince others by logic or by appeal to self-interest. We are all salespeople, or at least we should be, no matter what form of service we are rendering or what sort of goods we are offering.

The ability to negotiate with other people without friction and argument is the outstanding quality of all successful people. Observe those nearest you and notice how few there are who understand this art of tactful negotiation. Observe, also, how successful are the few who understand this art, despite the fact that they may have less education than those with whom they negotiate.

It is a knack that can be cultivated.

EDITOR'S NOTE

An advertising representative for a magazine received an angry phone call from one of his customers. The magazine's production department had placed incorrect information in a small ad and the client was furious. For ten minutes he yelled and screamed.

The ad rep was a master salesperson. He listened carefully to everything the client had to say. Then he interrupted with a simple statement: "You feel we hurt your business." Showing that he understood the customer's frustration immediately gave him the offensive.

He continued with, "I know you had big expectations from this ad and that you feel your money has been wasted. I'd like to make it up to you. With your permission, we will correct the ad and run it again, but this time twice as large at no charge."

The rep's words continued to reinforce the value of his magazine's service, while presenting the customer with a proposition that was difficult to refuse.

More significantly, however, the rep had gotten the customer to agree to a much larger ad. Of course, the first time it ran, the customer paid nothing for it. But the rep knew that once the customer experienced the business that the larger ad created, he would never go back to a small one.

By exercising self-control in his dealings with an irate customer, the ad rep turned a potential disaster into a positive opportunity.

NEGOTIATIONS REQUIRE SELF-CONTROL

The art of successful negotiation grows out of patient and painstaking self-control. Notice how easily the successful salesperson exercises self-control when handling an impatient customer. The salesperson may be boiling inside, but you will see no evidence of it in manner or words.

That person has acquired the art of tactful negotiation.

A single frown of disapproval or a single word denoting impatience will often spoil a sale. Successful salespeople exercise self-control, and as a reward they set their own salary and choose their own position.

To watch those who have acquired the art of successful negotiation is an education in itself. Watch the public speakers who have acquired this art; notice the firmness of step as they mount the platform; observe the firmness of voice as they begin to speak; study their facial expressions as they sweep the audience with the mastery of their arguments. These are people who have learned how to negotiate without friction.

Study those physicians who have acquired this art, as they walk into the sick room and greet their patients with a smile. The bearing, the tone of voice, the look of assurance, clearly identify them as professionals who have acquired the art of successful negotiation. And their patients will tell you it makes them feel better the moment such a doctor enters the sick room.

Watch the managers or supervisors who have acquired this art, and observe how their very presence spurs the employees to greater effort and inspires them with confidence and enthusiasm.

Watch the lawyer who has acquired this art, and observe how he or she commands the respect and attention of the court. There is something about the tone of voice, the posture, the expression, that causes opponents to suffer by comparison.

All of this is predicated upon self-control. And self-control is the result of thought control!

Deliberately place in your own mind the sort of thoughts that you wish to have there, and keep out of your mind those thoughts that others place there through suggestion, and you will become a person of self-control.

This privilege of stimulating your mind with suggestions and thoughts of your own choosing is your prerogative, and if you will exercise this right there is nothing within the bounds of reason that you cannot attain.

Losing your temper, and with it your case, or your argument, or your sanity, marks you as one who has not yet familiarized themselves with the fundamentals upon which self-control is based. And chief of these fundamentals is the privilege of choosing the thoughts that will dominate your mind.

A student in one of my classes once asked how one went about controlling one's thoughts when in a state of intense anger.

I replied: "In exactly the same way you would change your manner and the tone of your voice if you were in a heated argument with a member of your family and you heard the doorbell ring, warning that company had arrived. You would control yourself because you would desire to do so."

If you have ever been in a similar predicament, where you found it necessary to cover up your real feelings and change the expression on your face quickly, you know how easily it can be done. You also know that it can be done because one wants to do it.

Behind all achievement, behind all self-control, behind all thought control, is that magic something called desire.

It is no misstatement of fact to say that you are limited only by the depth of your desires. When your desires are strong enough, you will appear to possess superhuman powers to achieve. No one has ever explained this strange phenomenon of the mind, and perhaps no one ever will, but if you doubt that it exists, you have but to experiment and be convinced.

If you were in a building that was on fire, and all the doors and windows were locked, chances are that you would develop sufficient strength with which to break down the average door, because of your intense desire to free yourself.

If you desire to acquire the art of successful negotiation, as you undoubtedly will when you understand its significance in relation to your achievement of your definite chief aim, you will do so, providing your desire is intense enough.

Chapter 8

IMAGINATION

EDITOR'S NOTE

The first section of the following chapter is excerpted and adapted from **Law of Success,** *Volume II, Lesson Six.*

Perhaps there is no field of endeavor in which imagination plays such an important part as it does in salesmanship. The master salesperson sees the merits of the goods he or she sells, or the service they are rendering, in their own imagination, and if they fail to do so they will not make the sale.

A few years ago a sale was made which is said to have been the most far-reaching and important sale of its kind. The object of the sale was not merchandise but the freedom of a man who was confined in the Ohio penitentiary.

It began when I was invited to speak before the inmates of that penitentiary. When I stepped upon the platform I saw in the audience a man whom I had known as a successful businessman more than ten years previously.

That man was Butler R. Storke, whose pardon I later secured, and the story of whose release had been spread across the front page of practically every newspaper in the United States. Perhaps you will recall it.

After I had completed my address, I interviewed Mr. Storke and found out that he had been sentenced for forgery for a period of twenty years. After he told me his story, I said, "I will have you out of here in less than sixty days!"

With a forced smile he replied, "I admire your spirit but question your judgment. Why, do you know that at least twenty influential men have tried every means at their command to get me released, without success? It can't be done!"

I suppose it was that last remark—"It can't be done!"—that had challenged me to show him that it could be done. I returned to New York City and requested that my wife pack her trunks and get ready for an indefinite stay in the city of Columbus, where the Ohio penitentiary is located.

I had a definite purpose in mind! That purpose was to get Mr. Storke out of the Ohio penitentiary. Not only did I have in mind securing his release, but I intended to do it in such a way that it would reflect credit upon all who helped to bring it about.

Not once did I doubt that I would bring about his release, for no salesman can make a sale if he doubts that he can do it. My wife and I returned to Columbus and took up permanent headquarters.

The next day I called on the governor of Ohio and stated the object of my visit in about these words:

"Governor, I have come to ask you to release Mr. Storke from the Ohio penitentiary. I have sound reason for asking his release, and I hope you will give him his freedom at once, but I have come prepared to stay until he is released, no matter how long that may be.

"During his time in prison, Mr. Storke has launched a correspondence school in the Ohio penitentiary, as you of course know. He has influenced 1,729 of the 2,518 prisoners of the Ohio penitentiary to take up courses of instruction. He has managed to beg sufficient textbooks and lesson materials with which to keep these men at work on their lessons, and he has done this without a penny of expense to the state of Ohio. The warden and the chaplain of the penitentiary tell me that he has carefully observed the prison rules. Surely a man who can influence 1,729 prisoners to turn their efforts toward self-betterment cannot be a very bad sort of fellow.

"I have come to ask you to release Mr. Storke because I wish to place him at the head of a prison school that will give the 160,000 inmates of the other penitentiaries of the United States a chance to profit by his influence. I am prepared to assume full responsibility for his conduct after his release.

"That is my case, but before you give me your answer, I want you to know that I am not unmindful of the fact that your enemies will probably criticize you if you release him. In fact, if you release him it may cost you many votes if you run for office again."

With his fist clenched and his broad jaw set firmly, Governor Vic Donahey of Ohio said: "If that is what you want with Mr. Storke I will release him if it costs me five thousand votes. However, before I sign the pardon I want you to see the Clemency Board and secure its favorable recommendation. I want you also to secure the favorable recommendation of the warden and the chaplain of the Ohio penitentiary. You know that a governor is amenable to the court of public opinion, and these gentlemen are the representatives of that court."

The sale had been made! And the whole transaction had required less than five minutes.

The next day I returned to the governor's office, accompanied by the chaplain of the Ohio penitentiary, and notified the governor that the Clemency Board, the warden, and the chaplain all joined in recommending the release. Three days later the pardon was signed and Mr. Storke walked through the big iron gates, a free man.

I have cited the details to show you that there was nothing difficult about the transaction. The groundwork for the release had all been prepared before I came on the scene. Mr. Storke had done that, by his good conduct and the service he had rendered those 1,729 prisoners. When he created the world's first prison correspondence-school system, he created the key that unlocked the prison doors for himself.

Why then had the others who asked for his release failed to secure it? They failed because they used no imagination!

Perhaps they asked the governor for Mr. Storke's release on the grounds that his parents were prominent people, or on the grounds that he was a college graduate and not a bad sort of fellow. But they failed to supply the governor of Ohio with a sufficient motive to justify him in granting a pardon.

Before I went to see the governor I went over all the facts, and in my own imagination I saw myself in the governor's place and made up my mind what sort of a presentation would appeal most strongly to me if I were in his place.

When I asked for Mr. Storke's release, I did so in the name of the 160,000 unfortunate men and women inmates of the prisons of the United States who would enjoy the benefits of the correspondence-school system that he had created. I said nothing about his prominent parents. I said nothing about my friendship with him during former years. I said nothing about his being a deserving fellow. All these matters might have been used as sound reasons for his release, but they seemed insignificant when compared with the bigger and sounder reason that his release would be of help to 160,000 other people who would feel the influence of his correspondence-school system after his release.

And that was imagination. It was also salesmanship.

There were two important factors entering into Mr. Storke's release. The first was that he had supplied the material for a good case before I took it in charge, and the second was that before I called on the governor I had so completely convinced myself that I had a right to ask for Mr. Storke's release that I had no difficulty presenting my case effectively.

The governor could tell, long before I had stated my mission, that I knew I had a good case. If my mind did not telegraph this thought directly to his mind, then the look of self-confidence in my eyes and the positive tone of my voice made obvious my belief in the merits of my case.

I did nothing except use my imagination as an assembly room in which to piece together the factors out of which the sale was made. I did nothing except that which any salesperson with imagination could have done.

There are endless millions of approaches to every problem, but there is only one best approach. Find this one best approach and your problem is easily solved. No matter how much merit your goods may have, there are millions of wrong ways in which to offer them. Your imagination will assist you in finding the right way.

In your search for the right way to offer your merchandise or your services, you are once again reminded of this peculiar trait of mankind: People will grant favors that you request for the benefit of a third person when they would not grant them if requested for your benefit.

I had asked the governor to release Mr. Storke not as a favor to me, and not as a favor to Mr. Storke, but for the benefit of the 160,000 unfortunate inmates of the prisons of America.

Salespeople of imagination always offer their wares in such terminology that the advantages of those wares to the prospective purchaser are obvious. It is seldom that anyone makes a purchase of merchandise or renders another a favor just to accommodate the salesperson. It is a prominent trait of human nature that prompts us all to do that which advances our own interests.

To be perfectly plain, people are selfish!

To understand the truth is to understand how to present your case, whether you are asking for the release of someone from prison or offering for sale some commodity. In your own imagination, plan the presentation of your case so that the strongest and most impelling advantages to the buyer are made clear. This is imagination.

EDITOR'S NOTE

The following is excerpted from material in **Law of Success**, *Volume II, Lesson Six.*

A few years ago I received a letter from a young man who had just graduated from a business college and he wanted to secure employment in my office. With his letter he sent a crisp ten-dollar bill that had never been folded. The letter read as follows:

> I have just finished a commercial course in a first-class business college and I want a position in your office because I realize how much it would be worth to a young man, just starting out on his business career, to have the privilege of working under the direction of a man like you.
>
> If the enclosed ten-dollar bill is sufficient to pay for the time you would spend in giving me my first week's instructions, I want you to accept it. I will work the first month without pay and you may set my wages after that at whatever I prove to be worth.
>
> I want this job more than I ever wanted anything in my life and I am willing to make any reasonable sacrifice to get it.
>
> Very cordially . . .

This young man got his chance in my office. His imagination gained for him the opportunity that he wanted, and before his first month had expired, the president of a life insurance company who heard of this incident offered the young man a job as executive assistant at a substantial salary. He is today an official at one of the largest life insurance companies in the world.

EDITOR'S NOTE

Following are a number of true stories, excerpted from **Think and Grow Rich: The 21ˢᵗ-Century Edition,** *that illustrate how important imagination is in selling an idea. We begin with two stories that Napoleon Hill loved to tell in his lectures, and following that are a group of more contemporary stories. As you read, bear in mind that in every case imagination plays two separate roles: no matter how imaginative the basic idea was, that idea still had to be sold in a way that required just as much imagination.*

At the age of forty—an age at which the average man or woman begins to think they are too old to start anything new—James J. Hill was still working as a telegraph operator, at a salary of thirty dollars per month. He had no capital and he had no influential friends with capital. But he did have something more powerful than either—he had imagination.

In his mind's eye he saw a great railway system that would penetrate the undeveloped northwest and unite the Atlantic and Pacific oceans. So vivid was his imagination that he was also able to make others see the advantages of such a railway system. I would emphasize the part of the story that most people never mention—that Hill's Great Northern Railway system became a reality in his own imagination first.

This railroad was built with steel rails and wooden cross-ties, just as most other railroads are built, and these things were paid for with capital that was secured in very much the same manner that capital for all railroads is secured. But if you want the real story of James J. Hill's success, you must go back to that little country railway station where he worked at thirty dollars a month, and there pick up the little threads that he wove into a mighty railroad, with materials no more visible than the thoughts that he organized in his imagination.

What a mighty power is imagination, the workshop of the mind, in which thoughts are woven into railroads, skyscrapers, mills, factories, and all manner of material wealth.

THE ENCHANTED KETTLE

In the late 1880s an old country doctor drove to town, hitched his horse, quietly slipped into a drugstore by the back door, and began "dickering" with the young drug clerk.

For more than an hour, behind the prescription counter, the old doctor and the clerk talked in low tones. Then the doctor left. He went out to the buggy and brought back a large, old-fashioned kettle, a big wooden paddle (used for stirring the contents of the kettle), and deposited them at the back of the store.

The clerk inspected the kettle, reached into his inside pocket, took out a roll of bills, and handed it over to the doctor. The roll contained exactly five hundred dollars—the clerk's entire savings!

The doctor handed over a small slip of paper on which was written a secret formula. The words on that small slip of paper were worth a king's ransom. But not to the doctor. Those magic words were needed to start the kettle to boiling, but neither the doctor nor the young clerk knew what fabulous fortunes were destined to flow from that kettle.

What the clerk really purchased was an idea!

The old kettle and the wooden paddle, and the secret message on a slip of paper, were incidental. The miracle of that kettle only began to take place after the new owner mixed with the secret instructions an ingredient of which the doctor knew nothing.

Read on and discover what it was that the young man added to the secret message, which caused the kettle to overflow with gold. Here you have a story of facts stranger than fiction—facts that began in the form of an idea.

Just look at the vast fortunes of gold this idea has produced. It has paid, and still pays, huge fortunes to men and women all over the world who distribute the contents of the kettle to millions of people.

That old kettle is now one of the world's largest consumers of sugar, thus providing jobs to thousands of men and women engaged in growing sugar cane and in refining and marketing sugar.

The old kettle consumes, annually, millions of bottles *[and cans]*, providing jobs to huge numbers of workers.

The old kettle gives employment to an army of clerks, stenographers, copywriters, and advertising experts throughout the nation. It has brought fame and fortune to scores of artists who have created magnificent pictures describing the product.

The old kettle has converted Atlanta, which was a small southern city, into the business capital of the South, where it now benefits, directly or indirectly, every business and practically every resident of the city. The influence of this idea now benefits every civilized country in the world, pouring out a continuous stream of gold to all who touch it.

Gold from the kettle built and maintains one of the most prominent colleges of the South, where thousands of young people receive the training essential for success.

Whoever you are, wherever you may live, whatever your occupation, just remember, every time you see the words *Coca-Cola,* that its vast empire of wealth and influence grew out of a single idea. And that idea—the mysterious ingredient the drug clerk, Asa Candler, mixed with the secret formula—was . . . imagination!

EDITOR'S NOTE

Harlan Sanders, too, had a recipe and a magic kettle. Actually, his kettle was a pressure cooker, but neither his cooker nor his recipe of eleven herbs and spices would be mentioned here if he didn't also have imagination.

Harlan Sanders owned and operated a successful motel and café in Corbin, Kentucky. Then when the new interstate highway came through it bypassed Sanders' location. In a short time his business went broke, leaving him with little more than his recipe for fried chicken and a way to make it quickly in a pressure cooker.

At sixty-two years of age, the Colonel, as people called him, had to find a new way to make a living. That's when the magic ingredient, imagination, came in. He decided he wasn't going to sell fried chicken anymore; instead, he would sell his method for making it. He packed his recipe and cooker into the back of his car and hit the road to demonstrate his fried chicken to other restaurant owners. In the first two years he managed to sell five franchises. Two years later he'd sold two hundred. Four years later he was up to six hundred locations when he was approached by an investment group to sell his company.

Recognizing that the magic wasn't just in the kettle or the recipe, the new owners asked Colonel Sanders to stay on as spokesman for the company, which he did until his death in 1980. Today there are almost twelve thousand KFC locations in more than eighty countries, with sales of nearly $10 billion a year.

Debbie Fields was a twenty-year-old housewife who loved to bake cookies. She had no formal education and no business experience, but she had a recipe and an imaginative idea that people would like to buy fresh, hot, soft cookies from a walk-up store.

The businesspeople and bankers she approached told her she was crazy, but she and her husband continued to pitch her idea to banker after banker until they finally wore one down enough to give Debbie Fields a loan to open a store in Palo Alto, California. By noon on her first day she still hadn't sold a cookie, so she went out into the street and gave away samples. That did it. Her walk-in-try-a-sample cookie store took off.

Today Mrs. Fields' stores are all across America, Harvard Business School uses her methods as a case study in efficiency, and Debbie Fields has become a bestselling author, an in-demand motivational speaker, and a television personality.

Wally "Famous" Amos was a Los Angeles talent agent who copied a cookie recipe off the back of a bag of Nestlé's Chocolate Chips. He made a few changes to personalize the recipe and started to give out his version of homemade cookies as a sort of calling card.

His clients and business associates liked them so much that Wally finally decided to quit show business and open a store. He did it with a Hollywood agent's flair. He opened on Sunset Boulevard, with two thousand invitations, a red carpet, and celebrities. With the same flair, he put his picture on the bag, filled the bags with cookies, and started selling them to exclusive department stores and specialty shops.

Just ten years later, Famous Amos Cookies was a $10 million business.

Ray Kroc was over fifty and selling milkshake mixers when he heard about a hamburger stand in California, owned by Dick and Mac McDonald, that was doing great business. So he packed his car and headed to San Bernardino to check it out.

What he saw was a sit-down restaurant that had a limited menu featuring a good hamburger recipe, and they were serving them faster than any place he'd ever seen. Figuring that if there were more places like this he could sell them a lot of milkshake mixers, Kroc pitched the McDonald brothers on the idea of opening some more McDonald's. They were interested but they didn't know who they could get to open the new restaurants.

This time it was a recipe and a magic griddle, but it still needed the extra ingredient—imagination. On the spot, Ray Kroc offered to go into business with them and open the restaurants himself. According to the signs on the Golden Arches, Ray Kroc's imagination paid off in billions of hamburgers sold.

In 1982 Howard Schultz went to work as the director of marketing for a small coffee importer-wholesaler called Starbucks which had only one location, in Seattle's Pike Place Market.

While on a trip to Italy, Schultz got the idea that the coffee-bar culture he saw in Milan could be transposed to the downtown Seattle scene. He convinced the company to try it. His coffeehouse idea was such a success that Schultz went out and raised the money to buy the company. Five years after he'd joined Starbucks he was CEO of a company that had seventeen locations.

Fifteen years later, Schultz's coffeehouse culture was on just about every corner of America, and there were more than seven thousand Starbucks worldwide.

As a final example in these stories about imagination and selling, we offer Paul Newman's salad dressing. Now, it would seem that it doesn't take much imagination or sales ability for a big celebrity to put his name on a product, and that's what Newman thought too. But when he and his partner, A. E. Hotchner, pitched their salad-dressing idea to companies that specialize in marketing foods, nobody was interested unless they would personally put up about $1 million for the first year's operations. According to Newman and Hotchner's book, **Shameless Exploitation,** *they found out that almost all celebrity products in the food business have been disastrous failures and now nobody would touch them.*

So when it came to marketing salad dressing, even Paul Newman's big name wasn't the magic they needed. And unless they were willing to put up a ridiculous amount, money wasn't the magic either. The magic would have to be in the imaginative way they would convince the right people to help them and in having the perseverance to stick with it until they succeeded. And just like most everyone with an idea, they were told they were crazy to try it. They were turned down by bottling companies that wouldn't do small runs and they were rejected by distributors who wouldn't take a chance on another celebrity product.

In the end it was one supermarket owner, Stew Leonard, who helped hook them up with the right suppliers. But even that wouldn't have been enough if Stew Leonard hadn't had enough imagination to see the possibilities and agree to put Newman's Own Salad Dressing on the shelves in his store. Fifteen years later Newman's Own Brands was a $100 million company (which gives all profits to charity).

IMAGINATION SELLS

You will never know what your capacity is for achievement until you learn how to mix your efforts with imagination. The products of your hands, minus imagination, will yield you but a small return. But those same hands, when properly guided by imagination, can be made to earn you all the material wealth you can use.

If you are one of those who believe that hard work and honesty alone will bring riches, you can forget it! It is not true. Riches, when they come in huge quantities, are never the result of hard work alone. Riches come, if they come at all, in response to definite demands based on the application of definite principles—and not by chance or luck.

Generally speaking, an idea is a thought that prompts you to action because it appeals to your imagination. All master salespeople know that ideas can be sold where merchandise cannot. Ordinary salespeople do not know this. That is why they are "ordinary."

A publisher of low-priced books made a discovery that has been worth much to publishers. He learned that many people buy titles, and not the contents, of books. By merely changing the name of one book that was not moving, his sales of that book jumped upward more than a million copies. The inside of the book was not changed in any way. He merely ripped off the cover and put on a new cover with a title that had "box-office" appeal.

That, as simple as it may seem, was an idea. It was imagination. There is no standard price on ideas. The creator of ideas sets his or her own price, and, if they are smart, they get it.

EDITOR'S NOTE

For those readers who think that replacing the cover of a book is just too simple, or that they couldn't do it anyway because they're not book publishers, the editors would point out that if you had had that simple idea before the publisher did, he probably would have been glad to sell you those failed books at pennies on the dollar. Then you could have been the one to change the cover, and suddenly you would have been the publisher of a bestseller. However, the idea of replacing the covers wouldn't have meant a thing if you didn't also have ideas about how to market, promote, and sell that flashy new cover. And that is Hill's point. Coca-Cola was a recipe, a creative idea, but it would have stayed just a recipe if Asa Candler hadn't also had other creative ideas to market it and the faith in himself to carry through on those ideas.

Spence Silver was a chemist working for 3M when, by accident, he created a glue that wasn't very sticky. Needless to say, 3M was not much interested in a glue that didn't stick, and Silver's invention was shelved as a failure. But Silver liked his glue, so for five years he kept demonstrating it to anyone who would listen.

Nobody did, until Arthur Fry, who worked in the tape division at 3M, found that when he was at choir practice he kept losing his place in the hymnal because the pieces of paper he used to mark his place slipped down or fell out of the book. A little of Silver's not-very-sticky-glue on the slips of paper and they stayed where he wanted them, then peeled off easily when he was done. That was the eureka moment. They had just invented the world's best bookmark: Post-its.

But that's not the end of the story, or the end of the imaginative ideas that were needed to make Post-its happen. Fry would also need perseverance. First he had to convince the engineers to solve production problems, and to do it he knocked a hole in his basement wall so he could install a prototype of the production equipment. He stuck with it, and finally, two years later, 3M gave the project to their marketing department. The marketing experts put together ads and brochures selling this "sticky notepad" idea, and rolled it out in a four-city test. The results were a disaster. Nobody "got" it, so nobody bought it. Who would pay money for scratch paper?

The Post-it project was about to be scrapped when Geoffrey Nicholson and Joseph Ramey added their imaginations. Like Silver and Fry, Nicholson and Ramey had faith in the idea because they saw how people in their own office loved these sticky pieces of paper once they started working with them. So Nicholson and Ramey went to Richmond, Virginia, one of the four test cities that had failed, and they went up and down the business district, going into offices and giving pads of Post-its to receptionists, secretaries, and anyone else who would listen.

Whereas 3M's conventional marketing machinery had failed, giving Post-its to the people who would actually use them did the trick. Once those Richmond officeworkers started to use Post-its, it didn't seem like a bad idea at all to pay for scratch paper. They "got" it and they bought it. The Richmond test turned from failure to success, and soon Post-its were sticking to everything around the world.

Here is another simple idea that imagination and salesmanship turned into success. This story began with a man whose problem was just the opposite of Spence Silver's. He had something that stuck too well.

George de Mestrel was a Swiss mountaineer who went hunting one day with his dog. When they got home they were both covered with burrs. The burrs were so difficult to remove that de Mestrel put them under a magnifying glass to learn why. He saw that they were covered with tiny hooks which attached themselves to fur and fabric. That was when the flash hit: If burrs stuck where you didn't want them, why couldn't you put tiny hooks on things so they would stick where you did want them?

Like everyone else mentioned in this book, de Mestrel had an imaginative idea. But that was just the beginning. He also had the faith in himself to keep going when people laughed at his idea, which many did, until he eventually found a French textile plant that would help him do what he wanted. However, even when they finally worked out a way to use cotton fabric to make what they called "locking tape," they couldn't afford to mass-produce it. And that's when de Mestrel accidentally discovered that when you sew nylon under infrared light, it naturally made little hooks. Now that they could manufacture it economically, all they needed was a name. One side was fuzzy like velvet and the other side was crochet, the French word for **hook***. Take half "vel" and half "cro," combine it with imagination, the result is Velcro, and a Swiss mountaineer becomes a business tycoon.*

Clarence Saunders was a grocery clerk in a small southern retail store. One day he was standing with a tray in his hands, waiting his turn in a cafeteria. He had never earned more than twenty dollars a week before then and no one had ever noticed anything about him that indicated unusual ability, but something took place in his mind, as he stood in the line of waiting people, that put his imagination to work. That was when he came up with the idea that this same self-serve concept should also work at the grocery store.

Clarence Saunders took the idea to his boss. Naturally, his boss told him he was crazy. So Saunders quit his job, went out and did what he needed to do to raise the money, and he opened the first self-serve grocery store. He called it Piggly-Wiggly, and Clarence Saunders, the twenty-dollar-a-week grocery clerk, rapidly became the multimillion-dollar chain-store groceryman of America.

Sylvan Goldman was the owner of a number of Piggly-Wiggly stores in Oklahoma, and like any good businessman he spent a lot of time watching his customers go up and down the aisles putting their choices into their baskets or net shopping bags. One night, while trying to figure how to get his customers to buy more at one time, he found himself staring at a basket sitting on the seat of a wooden folding chair. Eureka! He called in his mechanic, Fred Young, they put some wheels on the bottom of the legs, added another basket below the seat, and the shopping cart was born.

As this edition is being readied for publication there are about 35 million shopping carts in America, and approximately 1.25 million new carts are sold each year.

Thomas Stemberg was another supermarket executive who watched his customers as they shopped. By this time shopping carts were well established in supermarkets, and it was because his customers were pushing shopping carts up and down the aisles that he got his flash of inspiration. He was so sure of his idea that he convinced another supermarket executive, Leo Kahn, to join him. Together they took the supermarket concept, applied it to selling office supplies, and in 1986 opened their first store in Brighton, Massachusetts. They called it Staples.

In 1989 they took the company public, and ten years later there were more than 1,000 Staples stores, with revenues exceeding $7 billion.

We'll end this Editor's Note with another set of connected stories which make the point that sometimes the most imaginative part of marketing is in the timing.

If you were to go shopping in the late 1800s it usually meant bartering with a merchant who would then have to get the goods from storage shelves kept behind the counter. In the 1870s fixed pricing was just starting to be used by storekeepers. Merchants were trying the idea by setting out a table of merchandise that was all priced the same, usually five cents.

Frank Winfield Woolworth was a clerk in a general store and he convinced the storeowner to let him try the five-cent-table idea. Although it worked, the owner wasn't impressed. So Woolworth borrowed $350 from his boss, and in 1879 opened his first Five Cents Store in Utica, New York. It was an entire store full of goods that all cost a nickel. A year later he had four stores, and the fourth one, in Lancaster, Pennsylvania, was the first that he named F. W. Woolworth's Five and Ten Cents Store. Twenty years later he had 238 stores. By the time of his death in 1919, there were over 1,000 F. W. Woolworth locations, he had established the first nationwide chain of general-merchandise stores, and he had built the tallest building in New York City as his headquarters.

The Woolworth company stayed true to the original idea and didn't carry any merchandise that cost more than a dime until 1932, when the top price was raised to twenty cents. But as times changed, the fixed-price was dropped, the merchandise became more varied, and the company kept growing until it had over 8,000 stores worldwide, selling everything from notions to appliances and furniture. Then in the 1960s something started to happen. The mood of America was changing but the Woolworth stores weren't. And that was when, in 1962, Sam Walton opened the first Wal-Mart in Rogers, Arkansas.

Walton got into the retail business after the Second World War, when his father-in-law loaned him the money to buy a franchised Butler Brothers store in Bentonville, Arkansas. By 1962 Sam and his brother Bud owned 16 variety stores in Arkansas, Missouri, and Kansas. It was in these stores that Sam Walton first started adding the magic ingredient of imagination. In addition to his flair for promotion, Sam tried new approaches to the way household goods and general merchandise could be sold at retail. He insisted on clean, well-lighted interiors and he introduced the concept of self-service, with aisles wide enough for shopping carts and checkout counters at the front of the store. He also started buying direct from manufacturers, and he created profit-sharing plans that kept his family of employees loyal, hardworking, and neighborly.

In 1962 he incorporated those and other imaginative ideas when he opened the first Wal-Mart store. The basic magic was that he sold brand-name merchandise at discount prices, but there was also magic in the way he kept a friendly hometown feel to his store even though it was what is now called a big-box store.

Sam Walton's Wal-Mart store was a success. So he just kept building and opening more of them. First in small towns and rural areas, then in larger towns, then big cities, and it wasn't long before he had a national chain. By 1992 when Sam Walton died, there were more than 1,700 Wal-Mart stores, it was the biggest retailer in the country, it employed more than 600,000 people, and Sam Walton was the richest man in America. In 2003 the stores numbered more than 3,200 in the U.S. and more than 1,100 in foreign countries, the company employed more than 1,300,000 people worldwide, and served more than one million customers a week.

Along the way, Woolworth's and other older retailers such as Kresge's tried to get on the bandwagon with their Woolco and Kmart stores, but they couldn't seem to get it right. They had given up their old five-and-dime identity to become higher-priced general retailers, and when Wal-Mart came along and redefined that part of the market, the others seemed to have run out of the kind of imagination they'd had in the beginning.

Now here's the twist to the story. David Gold was running a liquor store that he had inherited from his father. He noticed that whenever he put out a display of goods priced at 98 cents or $1.00 the goods would sell okay, but if his sign said 99 cents, the goods sold out in no time. He decided that he would open a store called The 99 Cents Only Store, where everything would be priced at 99 cents.

Sound familiar? Frank Woolworth's imaginative idea from 1879, which had been dropped at his namesake chain by the 1940s and 1950s, had just gotten a fresh shot of imagination from David Gold in 1982.

As usual, friends and family told him he was crazy, but David Gold went out to find suppliers who would sell him discontinued merchandise or overproduced products at a price low enough that he could offer them to the public at 99 cents. He found them. And they even had brand-name products of everything from hardware to pantihose, cleaning products, motor oil, kitchenware, cosmetics, electronics, toys, canned goods, frozen foods, cookies, fresh fruit, even gourmet foods—more than 5,000 items that he could sell for 99 cents and still make a profit!

David Gold opened his first well-lighted, brightly colored, green-and-fuchsia, wide-aisle store in Inglewood, California, in 1982. By 2003 he had 142 stores in California, Nevada, and Arizona, and he was listed on the Forbes 400 as having earned a personal fortune estimated at more than $650 million.

As Napoleon Hill wrote about the creation of Piggly-Wiggly, "Where in this story do you see the slightest indication of something that you could not duplicate? The plan, which made millions of dollars for its originator, was a very simple idea that anyone could have adopted, yet considerable imagination was required to put the idea to work in a practical sort of way. The more simple and easily adapted an idea is, the greater its value, as no one is looking for ideas that are involved with great detail or are in any way complicated."

IMAGINATION IS AT THE CENTER

This chapter on imagination can be thought of as the center of this course. Just as all the telephone wires lead to the exchange office for their source of power, every other lesson of the course leads to this lesson and makes use of the principle upon which it is based.

The materials out of which you build your definite chief aim are assembled and combined in your imagination. Self-confidence and initiative and leadership must be created in your imagination before they can become a reality, for it is in the workshop of your imagination that you will put the principle of autosuggestion into operation in creating these necessary qualities.

Just as the oak tree develops from the germ that lies in the acorn, and the bird develops from the germ that lies asleep in the egg, so will your material achievements grow out of the organized plans that you create in your imagination. First comes the thought; then organization of that thought into ideas and plans; then transformation of those plans into reality. The beginning, as you will observe, is in your imagination.

You will never have a definite purpose in life, you will never have self-confidence, you will never have initiative and leadership unless you first create these qualities in your imagination and see yourself in possession of them.

The imagination is both interpretative and creative in nature. It can examine facts, concepts, and ideas, and it can create new combinations and plans out of these.

EDITOR'S NOTE

Some of the most successful companies get started when an entrepreneur, drawing on his or her education, experience, and observations, takes an idea from one source and gives it a new application.

That is exactly what happened with Ruth Handler. She and her husband, along with another partner, had started a small manufacturing company which had evolved into toy manufacturing. The success of their business depended on coming up with new toy ideas.

Watching her young daughter at play, Ruth Handler noticed that she was fascinated with cutout books that featured teenage-girl or career-women paper dolls that she could cut out clothes for. She also knew that little girls loved to play dress-up in grown-up clothes. These ideas (drawn from Ruth Handler's education, experience, and observations) synthesized themselves in her imagination and came together as a new idea: Ruth Handler announced that they should make a lifelike teenage-girl doll. Not a paper doll but a real, three-dimensional, grown-up doll with a woman's figure, and they could also make grown-up clothes to fit so that girls could play dress-up with the doll.

*In honor of the source of inspiration, Ruth Handler named the new
doll after her daughter — Barbie.*

*As obvious as it seems now, until Ruth Handler, no one had the
imagination to make and market a doll that looked like a woman. And
certainly no one had ever made endless collections of tiny women's
fashions for a doll to wear.*

*Mary Kay Ash took the idea of women running their own businesses
and added the idea of door-to-door sales. Anita Roddick took the trend
of all-natural ingredients, combined it with cosmetics, and created The
Body Shop empire. Bernard Marcus and Arthur Blank took the concept
of the supermarket, combined it with hardware, and created Home
Depot. Thomas Stemberg and Leo Kahn did the same thing with office
supplies and launched Staples. Once the connections are made, it may
seem obvious, but making these supposedly obvious connections has
brought significant success to many people.*

You must learn to focus your imagination and to act on the ideas that
you develop. This is not an overnight process; a multimillion-dollar
marketing idea will not spring from your brain tomorrow just because
you will it. In most people, imagination is often handicapped by two
things.

First, it is not usefully focused. It flits from object to object, driven
by circumstance. Today your imagination may be stimulated by a movie
you saw, tomorrow by a newspaper headline, and the next day by a bit
of conversation you overhear. Its powers are scattered.

Or, second, it may be in thrall to the six basic fears, creating visions
of some rare and dreaded disease, a disaster at work, or a romantic
betrayal. In such situations its powers are at work, but only to your
detriment.

If you do begin to focus your imagination, it will not take long at
all for you to have many small ideas of surprising usefulness. As you
begin to apply these ideas, your confidence in your imagination and in
yourself will grow.

The most desirable and highest paid positions are those which imaginative people can create for themselves. Use your imagination to discover ways and means of stimulating business, and you may name your own salary.

Imagination brings the highest price of any ability. It always has a market and it has no limitations as to value. Business depressions do not destroy the market for imagination. In fact, bad times *increase* the demand for imagination. The world stands in need of men and women who will use their imaginations.

This is an age of rapid-fire change in business. It is an age that was made to order for men and women who use imagination. Not all of the new or best ways of doing business have yet been found. This need is your opportunity. Use your imagination and convert that opportunity into fortune. Create some new, unique idea that is sound—and sell it.

Take the shortcomings of the business in which you work and use your imagination to make it work better. Use your imagination to create a way to improve some part of any business that you are familiar with, and you will soon find a place for yourself.

Put your spare time to use by creating some plan that will improve your work or add to your employer's business. You can make yourself indispensable in this way. Indispensability commands a high price and permanency of employment at all times.

EDITOR'S NOTE

The following segment is excerpted and adapted from **Law of Success,** *Volume II, Lesson Six.*

There are two ways in which you can profit by imagination. You can develop this faculty in your own mind, or you can ally yourself with those who have already developed it. Andrew Carnegie did both. He not only made use of his own fertile imagination, but he gathered around him a group of specialists whose imaginations ran in numerous directions. In Mr. Carnegie's Master Mind alliance there were men whose imaginations were focused on the field of chemistry, others who specialized in finances, and still others whose imaginations were best suited to salesmanship.

It is said that Mr. Carnegie made more millionaires of his employees than any other employer in the steel business. Among those he made wealthy was Charles M. Schwab, who was known as the most able salesman on Mr. Carnegie's staff.

The fact that Schwab worked for someone else did not mean that he was less imaginative. In fact, it could be said that he displayed the soundest sort of imagination by his good judgment in allying himself with Mr. Carnegie. It is not a comedown to serve in the capacity of employee. To the contrary, it often proves to be the most profitable side of an alliance since not all of us are suited to assume the responsibility of directing others.

If you feel that your own imagination is not generating the kind of creative ideas you would like, read again the advice offered in the chapter on the Master Mind, and consider forming an alliance with someone whose imagination you respect, and who may prompt you to be more imaginative too.

EDITOR'S NOTE

There are numerous books and audiobooks specifically designed to help stimulate the imagination and create solutions to problems: **Super Creativity** *by Tony Buzan;* **The Artist's Way** *by Julia Cameron;* **Lateral Thinking, Six Thinking Hats,** and **Super Thinking,** *all by Edward De Bono;* **Drawing on the Right Side of the Brain** *by Betty Edwards;* **The Zen of Seeing** *by Frederick Franck;* **Writing Down the Bones** *by Natalie Goldberg;* **Peak Learning** *by Ronald Gross;* **Thinkertoys** *by Michael Michalko;* **Superlearning** *by Sheila Ostrander and Lynn Schroeder;* **Writing the Natural Way** *by Gabriele Rico;* **A Kick in the Seat of the Pants** *by R. von Oech. There are also numerous computer programs designed to stimulate new ideas and creativity.*

Chapter 9

SELF-CONFIDENCE

EDITOR'S NOTE

The first section of the following chapter is excerpted from **Law of Success**, *Volume I, Lesson Three.*

One of the greatest salesmen this country has ever seen was once a clerk in a newspaper office. It will be worth your while to analyze what part self-confidence played in the method through which he gained his title as "the world's leading salesman."

He was a timid young man with a more or less retiring sort of nature. He was one of those who believe it best to slip in by the back door and take a seat at the rear of the stage of life. One evening he heard a lecture on the subject of this lesson, self-confidence, and that lecture so impressed him that he left the lecture hall with a firm determination to pull himself out of the rut into which he had drifted.

He went to the business manager of the newspaper, asked for a position as an advertising salesman, and was put to work on a commission basis. Everyone in the office expected to see him fail, as this sort of salesmanship calls for the most positive type of sales ability. He went to his room and made out a list of certain merchants on whom he intended to call.

One would think that he would naturally have made up his list of the names of those whom he believed he could sell with the least effort, but he did nothing of the sort. He listed only the names of the merchants on whom other advertising salespeople had called without making a sale. His list consisted of only twelve names.

Before he made a single call he went to the city park, took out his list of twelve names, and read it over a hundred times, saying to himself as he did so, "You will purchase advertising space from me before the end of the month." Then he began to make his calls.

The first day he closed sales with three of the twelve "impossibilities." During the remainder of the week he made sales to two others. By the end of the month he had opened advertising accounts with all but one of the merchants on his list. For the ensuing month he made no sales because he made no calls, except on this one obstinate merchant.

Every morning when the store opened he was there to speak with this merchant and every morning the merchant said no. The merchant knew he was not going to buy advertising space, but this young man didn't know it. When the merchant said no, the young man did not hear it; he kept right on coming. On the last day of the month, after having told this persistent young man no for thirty consecutive times, the merchant said: "Look here, young man, you have wasted a whole month trying to sell to me. What I would like to know is why have you wasted your time?"

"Wasted my time nothing," he retorted, "I have been going to school and you have been my teacher. Now I know all the arguments that a merchant can bring up for not buying, and besides that I have been drilling myself in self-confidence."

Then the merchant said, "I will make a little confession of my own. I, too, have been going to school, and you have been my teacher. You have taught me a lesson in persistence that is worth money to me, and to show you my appreciation I am going to pay my tuition fee by giving you an order for advertising space."

And that was the way in which the Philadelphia North American's best advertising account was brought in. That one sale also marked the beginning of a reputation that has since made that same young man a millionaire. He succeeded because he deliberately charged his own mind with sufficient self-confidence to make that mind an irresistible force.

When he sat down to make up that list of twelve names, he did something that ninety-nine people out of a hundred would not have done—he selected the names of those whom he believed it would be hard to sell, because he understood that out of the resistance he would meet with in trying to sell them would also come strength and self-confidence.

SELF-CONFIDENCE BEGINS AT HOME

[The following is excerpted from **Law of Success**, *Volume I, Lesson Three.]*

From having analyzed more than 16,000 people, the majority of whom were married, I have learned something that may be of value. You have it within your power to send your spouse away to his or her work, business, or profession each day with a feeling of self-confidence that will carry them successfully over the rough spots of a day and bring them home again at night, smiling and happy.

A man I know well married a woman who had a set of false teeth. One day his wife dropped her teeth and broke the plate. The husband picked up the pieces and began examining them. He showed such interest in them that his wife said, "You could make a set of teeth like those if you made up your mind to do it."

This man was a farmer whose ambitions had never carried him beyond the bounds of his little farm until his wife made that remark. She walked over, laid her hand on his shoulder, and encouraged him to try his hand at dentistry. She finally coaxed him to make the start, and because of her encouragement and his self-confidence that grew from it, he became one of the most prominent and successful dentists in the state of Virginia. I know him well, for he is my father.

No one can foretell the possibilities of achievement available to the man or woman whose partner supports and encourages bigger and better endeavor. It is your right and your duty to encourage your mate until he or she finds an appropriate place in the world. You can induce your mate to put forth greater effort than can any other person in the world. Make him or her believe that nothing within reason is beyond reach and you will have rendered a service that will go a long way toward winning the battle of life.

One of the most successful men in his line in America gives entire credit for his success to his wife. When they were first married, she wrote a creed which he signed and placed over his desk. This is what it said:

> I believe in myself. I believe in those who work with me. I believe in my employer. I believe in my friends. I believe in my family. I believe that God will lend me everything I need with which to succeed if I do my best to earn it through faithful and honest service. I believe in prayer and I will never close my eyes in sleep without praying for divine guidance to the end that I will be patient with other people and tolerant with those who do not believe as I do. I believe that success is the result of intelligent effort and does not depend upon luck or sharp practices or double-crossing friends, fellow men, or my employer. I believe I will get out of life exactly what I put into it, therefore I will be careful to conduct myself toward others as I would want them to act toward me. I will not slander those whom I do not like. I will not slight my work no matter what I may see others doing.

> I will render the best service of which I am capable because I have pledged myself to succeed in life and I know that success

is always the result of conscientious and efficient effort. Finally, I will forgive those who offend me because I realize that I shall sometimes offend others and I will need their forgiveness.

Signed . . . .

The woman who wrote this creed was a practical psychologist of the first order. With the influence and the guidance of such a marriage partner, any man or woman could achieve noteworthy success.

Analyze this creed and you will observe how freely the personal pronoun is used; it starts off with the affirmation of self-confidence, which is perfectly appropriate. You could not make this creed your own without developing the positive attitude that would attract people who would aid you in your struggle for success.

This would be a splendid creed for every salesperson to adopt. Mere adoption, however, is not enough. You must practice it. Read it over and over until you know it by heart. Then repeat it at least once a day until you have literally transformed it into your mental makeup. Keep a copy of it in front of you as a daily reminder of your pledge to practice it. By doing so you will be making efficient use of the principle of autosuggestion as a means of developing self-confidence.

Never mind what anyone may say about your procedure. You know that any idea you firmly fix in your subconscious mind, by repeated affirmation, automatically becomes a plan or blueprint that an unseen power uses in directing your efforts toward the attainment of the objective named in the plan. Just remember that it is your business to succeed, and this creed, if mastered and applied, will go a long way toward helping you.

IF YOU THINK YOU ARE BEATEN, YOU ARE

[The following segment is excerpted and adapted from Law of Success, *Volume I, Lesson Three.]*

Henry Ford made millions of dollars each year because he believed in Henry Ford and transformed that belief into a definite purpose backed with a definite plan. The other machinists who worked with Ford during the early days of his career envisioned nothing but a weekly pay envelope. That was all they ever got because they demanded nothing out of the ordinary of themselves. If you want to get more, be sure to demand more of yourself. Notice that this demand is to be made on yourself.

Perhaps you have wondered why a few will advance to highly paid positions while others all around them, who have as much training and who seemingly perform as much work, do not get ahead. Select any two people of these two types and study them, and the reason why one advances and the other stands still will be quite obvious to you. You will find that those who advance believe in themselves, and they back their belief with such dynamic, aggressive action that others can recognize it in them. You will also notice that this self-confidence is contagious; it is impelling; it is persuasive; it attracts others.

You will also find that those who do not advance show clearly, by the look on their face, by the posture of their body, by the lack of briskness in their step, by the uncertainty with which they speak, that they lack self-confidence. No one is going to pay much attention to those who have no confidence in themselves. They do not attract others because their minds are a negative force that repels rather than attracts.

In no other field of endeavor does self-confidence, or the lack of it, play such an important part as in the field of sales, and one does not need to be a character analyst to determine, on first meeting, whether a salesperson possesses this quality. If you have it, the signs of its influence are written all over you. You inspire customers with confidence in you and in the goods you are selling the moment you speak.

This brings to mind a familiar poem which expresses a great psychological truth:

> If you think you are beaten, you are;
> If you think you dare not, you don't;
> If you like to win, but you think you can't,
> It is almost certain you won't.

If you think you'll lose, you've lost,
For out of the world we find
Success begins with a fellow's will—
It's all in the state of mind.

If you think you are outclassed, you are—
You've got to think high to rise.
You've got to be sure of yourself before
You can ever win a prize.

Life's battles don't always go
To the stronger or faster man;
But soon or late the man who wins
Is the man who thinks he can.

Commit this poem to memory and use it as a part of your working equipment in the development of your self-confidence.

THE MAN IN THE MIRROR

[The following is excerpted from **Law of Success,** *Volume I, Lesson Three.]*

Somewhere in your makeup there is a "subtle something" which, if it were aroused by the proper outside influence, would carry you to heights of achievement such as you have never before anticipated. Just as a master player can take hold of a violin and make it pour forth the most beautiful and entrancing strains of music, so is there some outside influence that can take hold of your mind and cause you to go forth into the field of your chosen endeavor and play a glorious symphony of success. No one knows what hidden forces lie dormant within you.

You, yourself, do not know your capacity for achievement, and you never will know until you come in contact with the particular stimulus that arouses you to greater action and extends your vision, develops your self-confidence, and moves you with a deeper desire to achieve.

It is not unreasonable to expect that some statement, some idea, or some stimulating word of this course will serve as the needed stimulus that will reshape your destiny and redirect your thoughts and energies along a pathway that will lead you, finally, to your coveted goal in life. It is strange but true that the most important turning points of life often come at the most unexpected times and in the most unexpected of ways.

I have in mind a typical example of this, and of what a person can accomplish when he or she awakens to a full understanding of the value of self-confidence. The incident to which I refer happened in the city of Chicago while I was engaged in the work of character analysis.

One day a homeless man presented himself at my office and asked for an interview. As I looked up from my work and greeted him, he said, "I have come to see the man who wrote this little book," and he removed from his pocket a copy of a book entitled *Self-Confidence*, which I had written many years previously.

"It must have been the hand of fate," he continued, "that slipped this book into my pocket yesterday afternoon, because I was about ready to go out there and punch a hole in Lake Michigan. I had about come to the conclusion that everything and everybody, including God, had it in for me, until I read this book. It gave me a new viewpoint and brought me the courage and the hope that sustained me through the night. I made up my mind that if I could see the man who wrote this book, he could help me get on my feet again. Now I am here and I would like to know what you can do for a man like me."

While he was speaking I had been studying him from head to foot and I am frank to admit that down deep in my heart I did not believe there was anything I could do for him, but I did not wish to tell him so. The glassy stare in his eyes, the lines of discouragement in his face, the posture of his body, the ten days' growth of beard on his face, the nervous manner about this man all conveyed to me the impression that he was hopeless, but I did not have the heart to tell him.

So I asked him to sit down and tell me his whole story. I asked him to be perfectly frank and to tell me, as nearly as possible, just what had brought him down to the ragged edge of life. I promised him that after I heard his entire story I would then tell him whether or not I could be of service to him.

He related his story, in lengthy detail, the sum and substance of which was this: He had invested his entire fortune in a small manufacturing business. When the World War began in 1914, it was impossible for him to get the raw materials necessary for the operation of his factory, and he therefore failed. The loss of his money broke his heart and so disturbed his mind that he left his wife and children and went to live on the streets. He had brooded over his loss until he reached the point at which he was contemplating suicide.

After he had finished his story, I said to him: "I have listened to you with a great deal of interest, and I wish that there was something I could do to help you. But there is absolutely nothing."

He became as pale as he will be when he is laid away in a coffin. He settled back in his chair and dropped his chin on his chest, as much as to say, "That settles it."

I waited for a few seconds, then said: "While there is nothing that I can do for you, there is a man in this building to whom I will introduce you, if you wish, who can help you regain your lost fortune and put you back on your feet again." These words had barely fallen from my lips when he jumped up, grabbed me by the hands, and said, "For God's sake, lead me to this man."

It was encouraging to note that he had asked this "for God's sake." This indicated that there was still a spark of hope within him, so I took him by the arm and led him out into the laboratory where my psychological tests in character analysis were conducted, and stood with him in front of what looked to be a curtain over a door. I pulled the curtain aside and uncovered a tall mirror in which he saw himself from head to foot. Pointing my finger at the glass, I said:

"There stands the man to whom I promised to introduce you. He is the only man in this world who can put you back on your feet again. And unless you sit down and become acquainted with that man, as you never became acquainted with him before, you might just as well go on over and 'punch a hole' in Lake Michigan, because you will be of no value to yourself or to the world until you know this man better."

He stepped over to the glass, rubbed his hands over his bearded face, studied himself from head to foot for a few moments, then stepped back, dropped his head, and began to weep. I knew that the lesson had been driven home.

I never expected to see him again, and I doubted that the lesson would be sufficient to help him regain his place in the world, because he seemed too far gone for redemption. He seemed to be not only down, but almost out.

A few days later I met this man on the street. His transformation had been so complete that I hardly recognized him. He was walking briskly, with his head tilted back. That old, shifting, nervous posture of his body was gone. He was dressed in new clothes from head to foot. He looked prosperous and he felt prosperous. He stopped me and related what had happened to bring about his rapid transformation from a state of abject failure to one of hope and promise.

"I was just on my way to your office," he explained, "to bring you the good news. I went out the very day that I was in your office, a down-and-out tramp, and despite my appearance I sold myself at a salary of $3,000 a year. Think of it, man, $3,000 a year! And my employer advanced me money enough to buy some new clothes, as you can see for yourself. He also advanced me some money to send home to my family, and I am once more on the road to success. It seems like a dream when I think that only a few days ago I had lost hope and faith and courage, and was actually contemplating suicide.

"I was coming to tell you that one of these days, when you are least expecting me, I will pay you another visit, and when I do I will be a successful man. I will bring with me a blank check, signed and made payable to you, and you may fill in the amount because you have saved me from myself by introducing me to myself—that self I never knew until you stood me in front of that mirror and pointed out the real me."

As he turned and departed into the crowded streets of Chicago, I saw, for the first time in my life, what strength and power and possibility lie hidden in the mind of the person who has never discovered the value of self-reliance. Then and there I made up my mind that I, too, would stand in front of that same mirror and point an accusing finger at myself for not having discovered the lesson that I had helped another to learn. I did stand before that same mirror, and as I did, I then and there fixed in my mind, as my definite purpose in life, the determination to help men and women discover the forces that lie sleeping within them. The book that you hold in your hands is evidence that my definite purpose is being carried out.

The man whose story I have related here is now president of one of the largest and most successful concerns of its kind in America, with a business that extends from coast to coast and from Canada to Mexico.

SELF-CONFIDENCE FORMULA

[The following is excerpted from **Law of Success,** *Volume I, Lesson Three.]*

We come now to the point at which you are ready to take hold of the principle of autosuggestion and make direct use of it in developing yourself into a positive, dynamic, self-reliant person. Copy the following formula, sign it, and commit it to memory:

1. I know that I have the ability to achieve the object of my definite purpose, therefore I demand of myself persistent, aggressive, and continuous action toward its attainment.

2. I realize that the dominating thoughts of my mind will eventually reproduce themselves in outward, bodily action and then gradually

transform themselves into physical reality. Therefore, I will concentrate my mind for thirty minutes daily on the task of thinking of the person I intend to be, by creating a mental picture of this person and then transforming that picture into reality through my actions.

3. I know that through the principle of autosuggestion, any desire that I persistently hold in my mind will eventually seek expression through some practical means of realizing it. Therefore, I shall devote ten minutes daily to demanding of myself the development of the factors named in the seventeen lessons of the *Law of Success* course.

4. I have clearly mapped out, and written down, a description of my definite purpose in life for the next five years. I have set a price on my services for each of these five years, a price that I intend to earn and receive through strict application of the principle of efficient, satisfactory service, which I will render in advance.

5. I fully realize that no wealth or position can long endure unless it is built upon truth and justice. Therefore, I will engage in no transaction that does not benefit all whom it affects. I will succeed by attracting to me the forces I wish to use and the cooperation of other people. I will induce others to serve me because I will first serve them. I will eliminate hatred, envy, jealousy, selfishness, and cynicism by developing love for all humanity, because I know that a negative attitude toward others can never bring me success. I will cause others to believe in me because I will believe in them and in myself.

6. I will sign my name to this formula, commit it to memory, and repeat it aloud once a day with full faith that it will gradually influence my entire life so that I will become a successful and happy worker in my chosen field of endeavor.

Signed . . . .

EDITOR'S NOTE

The following is taken from a live recording of Napoleon Hill addressing the assembled members of Napoleon Hill Associates. Because it is adapted from a direct transcription of the audio track, this story presents a wonderfully candid example of Napoleon Hill confirming, in his own words, how he used autosuggestion to set a definite chief aim and to build his self-confidence.

One morning in my New York headquarters, I received a telephone call from the president of the Newark Laundry Company. He asked me to come and talk with him about training his salesmen. Until then, I had never known that a laundry employed salesmen. Later, I learned that all his drivers operated independently and that they had to procure their own accounts and hold them. In order to do that, they had to know something about selling. It was a new field for me, and I made up my mind that I was going to get the account, come what may.

I decided to condition my mind before I went to Newark so that it would be impossible for me to come back without the sale.

I went into my office, closed the door, and asked the operator not to ring my phone until I came out. I sat down at my desk, then put my elbows on the desk and my head in my hands, and began to condition my mind. I said, "Napoleon, you are going to see this laundryman and you are not coming back until you make a sale."

I repeated that more than a hundred times, until the psychological moment arrived when I knew that I was going to make the sale, when I got the feeling that I had made a sale. To whom? Why, to myself.

Then I called in my sales manager, Jack Randall, and I said, "Jack, you've been hearing me talk about this business of conditioning the mind not to accept "no." Well, I'm going to take you over to Newark to demonstrate just exactly how it's done. We're going over to see the president of the Newark Laundry, and we are not coming back until we make a sale.

He said, "Now, just a minute. I have a family and I've got to come back."

I said, "I have a family too, and I am coming back, but I'm not coming back until we make a sale."

When we were introduced to the president, he said, "Gentlemen, come right in. It's a very warm day, and we'll go over to the Athletic Club for lunch in a nice air-conditioned room, and afterwards we will go into the library, sit down, and have no disturbance while we talk." Jack Randall looked over at me and winked, as if to say, "Boss, it's all in the bag." That's what he thought and that's what I thought too.

We went over there, and all during the luncheon this gentleman was telling what his problems were and how they came about. Someone had circulated the report among his customers that his work was not sanitary. It had reached the drivers, and they were losing one account after another.

While he was talking I was making a plan. I knew what had to be done. I told him what I thought was wrong, how it could be corrected, how long it would take, and how much it would cost. All the time that I was talking, he was smiling and nodding his head, and I could see from the expression on his face that he was buying every word I said. I was absolutely sure of myself.

After I stopped and came up for air for a few minutes, the laundry-man said, "Mr. Hill, I like your plan. I like it wonderfully well. I like you and I like your manager, but when I telephoned your office, I also telephoned two other gentlemen who were in the business of training salesmen and I made appointments with them too. The other two are coming here tomorrow. I've got to tell you that I think you've got it in the bag, but I've got to see the other two men first."

I looked over at Jack, who was just getting up from his chair, and I gave him such a cold look that he sat back down. He knew from my look that I had made up my mind that we were going to make a sale, and we weren't going anywhere until we did.

What would you have done if you had been in my place at that point?

Well, what I did was ignore what the laundryman said, and go right into the second phase of my sales talk. I had one or two other sales talks up my sleeve, so to speak, that I hadn't used in my first presentation. A good salesman always has other approaches, but he doesn't spring them all at one time.

I had been talking for about four to five minutes when I slowed down a bit again.

The laundryman jumped in and said, "Now, Mr. Hill, I'm still with you, and I think you've got the job, but, Mr. Hill, if you were in my place and you had made an engagement with two other men, what would you do?"

I said, "That's just exactly what I was waiting for you to ask. I'll tell you what I would do. I would telephone those other two gentlemen and tell them you have already employed Napoleon Hill, thank them for their consideration, and save them a trip over to your place."

He replied, "By gosh, that's exactly what I'll do."

EDITOR'S NOTE

And that is how Napoleon Hill used the autosuggestion techniques of visualization and positive affirmations to bolster his self-confidence and achieve his definite chief aim.

Chapter 10

INITIATIVE & LEADERSHIP

—————

EDITOR'S NOTE

The following section is adapted from material in **How to Sell Your Way Through Life** *combined with material from* **Law of Success**, *Volume II, Lesson Five.*

The reason why initiative and leadership are associated terms in this book is that leadership is essential for the attainment of success, and initiative is the very foundation on which this necessary quality of leadership is built. Initiative is that exceedingly rare quality which impels a person to do what ought to be done without being told to do it. Initiative is as essential to success as a hub is essential to a wheel.

One of the peculiarities of leadership is the fact that it is never found in those who have not acquired the habit of taking the initiative. Leadership is something that you must invite yourself into; it will never thrust itself upon you.

If you are a successful leader you are also an efficient salesperson. You have a pleasing personality, you are optimistic and enthusiastic, and you know how to transmit your enthusiasm and optimism to your followers. You get people to do things because they wish to do them for you. You are a self-starter, with self-confidence, who is not content to wait and see what happens. You are the one who takes the initiative and makes things happen.

Initiative means doing things without being told to do them. It means selecting a definite aim, then developing the plan needed to achieve that aim.

INITIATIVE IN ACTION

[The following section is excerpted from **Law of Success,** *Volume II, Lesson Five.]*

In 1916 I needed $25,000 *[the equivalent, at the beginning of the twenty-first century, of approximately a half-million dollars]* with which to create an educational institution, but I had neither the money nor sufficient collateral with which to borrow it through the usual banking sources. Did I bemoan my fate or think of what I might accomplish if some rich relative or Good Samaritan would come to my rescue by loaning me the necessary capital?

I did nothing of the sort! I did just what you will be advised, throughout this course, to do. First of all, I made the securing of this capital my definite chief aim. Second, I laid out a complete plan to transform this aim into reality. Backed by self-confidence and initiative, I proceeded to put my plan into action. But before the "action" stage of the plan had been reached, more than six weeks of study, effort, and thought were put into it. If a plan is to be sound it must be built of carefully chosen material.

I wanted this $25,000 in capital for the purpose of creating a school of advertising and salesmanship. Two things were necessary for the organization of such a school. One was the $25,000, which I did not have, and the other was the proper course of instruction, which I did have. My problem was to ally myself with some group who needed what I had, and who would supply the $25,000.

I needed to come up with a way to bring together several interested parties in such a way that each of these interests is greatly strengthened and each supports all the others, just as one link in a chain supports all the other links.

After I had done my research and laid out my plan, I presented it to the owner of a well-known and reputable business college which just then was finding they were up against tough competition for student enrollment.

My plan was presented in about these words:

Whereas, you have one of the most reputable business colleges in the city; and,

Whereas, you need some plan with which to meet the stiff competition in your field; and,

Whereas, your good reputation has provided you with all the credit you need; and,

Whereas, I have the plan that will help you meet this competition successfully, let us work together through a plan that will give you what you need and at the same time supply me with something that I need.

Then I proceeded to unfold my plan further, in these words:

I have written a very practical course on advertising and salesmanship. Having built this course out of my actual experience in training and directing salespeople, and my experience in planning and directing many successful advertising campaigns, I now have behind it plenty of evidence of its soundness.

If you will use your credit in helping market this course, I will place it in your business college as one of the regular departments of your curriculum and take entire charge of this newly created department. No other business college in the city will be able to meet your competition, because no other college has a course such as this. The advertising that you do in marketing this course will also serve to create the demand for your regular business course. You may charge to my department the entire amount that you spend for this advertising, leaving for you the accumulative advantage that will accrue to your other departments without cost to you.

Now, I suppose you will want to know where I will profit by this transaction, and I will tell you. I want you to enter into a contract with me in which it will be agreed that when the cash receipts from my department equal the amount you have paid out for advertising, my department and my course in advertising and salesmanship become my own, and I may have the privilege of separating this department from your school and running it under my own name.

The plan was agreeable and the contract was closed. (Please keep in mind that my definite purpose was to secure the use of $25,000 for which I had no security to offer.)

In a little less than a year, the business college had paid out slightly more than $25,000 for advertising and marketing my course. Meanwhile, my department had turned in tuition fees equaling the amount the college had spent, and I took the department over according to the terms of my contract.

This newly created department not only served to attract students for the other departments of the college, but at the same time, the tuition fees collected through this new department were sufficient to place it on a self-sustaining basis before the end of the first year.

So you can see that while the college did not loan me one penny of actual capital, it nevertheless supplied me with credit, which served exactly the same purpose.

I said that my plan was founded on a plan that would benefit all parties concerned. The benefit accruing to me was the use of the $25,000, which resulted in an established, independent business by the end of the first year. The benefit accruing to the college was the new students secured for its regular commercial and business course as a result of the money spent in advertising my department.

Today that business college is one of the most successful schools of its kind, and it stands as a monument of sound evidence with which to demonstrate the value of initiative and allied effort.

The master salesperson is essentially a leader who gets people to cooperate in a spirit of harmony by planting in their minds adequate motives. The master salesperson reaches his or her followers and influences them through their emotions as well as their reason.

All great leaders are masters of sales. And all master salespeople are great leaders. They understand the art of persuasion; they understand how to set up, in the minds of their followers, motives that will induce favorable, willing cooperation.

Master salespeople can sell anything they choose to sell because they have sufficient initiative to create markets. Moreover, they can sell one commodity, idea, plan, form of service, or motive just as easily as any other.

Great leaders and master salespeople use the same philosophy. They sell their followers or patrons whatever they choose to sell by establishing a relationship of confidence.

QUALITIES OF A LEADER

[The following is adapted from How to Sell Your Way Through Life.*]*

In applying initiative and leadership, certain definite steps are essential. The following are the most important of these steps:

1. Know definitely what you want.

2. Build a practical plan or plans for the achievement of that which you want, making use of the counsel and advice of your Master Mind group.

3. Surround yourself with an organization made up of people who have the knowledge and experience essential for carrying out your definite aim.

4. Have sufficient faith in yourself and your plans to envision your goal as a finished reality, even before you begin to carry out your plans.

5. Do not become discouraged, no matter with what obstacles you may meet. If one plan fails to work, substitute other plans until you have found the one that will work.

6. Do no guessing. Get the facts as the basis for all of your plans.

7. Do not be influenced by others to abandon your plans or your aim.

8. Have no set hours of labor. The leader must devote whatever hours are necessary for success.

9. Concentrate upon one thing at a time. You cannot dissipate thought and energy and still be efficient.

10. Whenever possible delegate to others the responsibility of details, but have a system for checking your subordinates to see that these details are accurately attended to. Hold yourself accountable at all times for carrying out all of your plans, bearing in mind that if subordinates fail, it is you yourself who has failed.

STRONG LEADERS MAKE PROMPT DECISIONS

The first step essential to the development of initiative and leadership is that of forming the habit of prompt and firm decision. The leader who hesitates between vague notions of what he or she wants to do or should do, generally ends by doing nothing.

If you are a leader who changes your mind often, you will soon lose the confidence of those you are leading. A natural tendency of human nature is a willingness to follow the person with great self-confidence. If you are not sure of yourself, how can you expect others to be sure of you? No one will want to follow you if you are not sure of yourself.

There are circumstances, of course, which call for slow deliberation and examination of facts before an intelligent decision can be reached. However, after all the available facts have been gathered and organized, there is no excuse for delaying decision, and the person who practices the habit of delay cannot become an effective leader unless this shortcoming is mastered.

HOW TO ELIMINATE PROCRASTINATION

[The following is adapted from How to Sell Your Way Through Life *combined with material from* Law of Success, *Volume II, Lesson Five.]*

First you must master the habit of procrastination and eliminate it from your makeup. This habit of putting off until tomorrow what you should have done last week or last year is gnawing at your very being, and you can accomplish nothing until you throw it off.

You can eliminate the habit of procrastination through the use of the methods taught in the chapter Autosuggestion. Begin by copying the following formula and put it in a conspicuous place in your room where you will see it as you retire at night and as you arise in the morning:

Having chosen _____ [insert your definite chief aim] as my life's work, I now understand it to be my duty to transform this aim into reality. Therefore, I will form the habit of taking some definite action each day that will carry me one step nearer the attainment of this chief aim.

I know that procrastination is a deadly enemy of all who would become leaders in any undertaking, and I will eliminate this habit from my makeup by:

1. Doing one definite thing each day, something that ought to be done, without anyone telling me to do it.

2. Looking around until I find at least one thing that I can do each day, that I have not been in the habit of doing, and that will be of value to others, without expectation of pay.

3. Telling at least one other person, each day, of the value of practicing this habit of doing something that ought to be done without being told to do it.

I know that the muscles of the body become stronger in proportion to the amount they are used. Therefore, I understand that the habit of initiative also becomes fixed in proportion to the extent that it is practiced.

I realize the place to begin developing the habit of initiative is in the small, commonplace things connected with my daily work. Therefore, I will go at my work each day as if I were doing it solely for the purpose of developing this necessary habit of initiative.

I understand that by practicing this habit of taking the initiative in connection with my daily work I will be not only developing that habit, but I will also be attracting the attention of those who will place greater value on my services as a result of this practice.

Signed . . . .

LEADERS DON'T SWEAT THE SMALL STUFF

[The following resumes from How to Sell Your Way Through Life.*]*

If you are an efficient leader you will never permit yourself to be loaded down with small details. One of the outstanding qualities of a leader is the ability to organize plans so that you are free at all times to place the weight of your personal effort wherever it is most needed. I have met and interviewed many of the most able industrial leaders of America. Not one of them ever seemed to be overworked, because in every case they knew when and how to delegate responsibility to others.

The leader who boasts of personally inspecting all the details of his or her business is either not an able leader or it is a very small business. "I haven't had time" is said to be the most dangerous sentence in the English language. Any person who makes such an admission confesses lack of ability as a leader. The real leader has time for everything necessary to successful leadership.

The stock excuse to justify not having selected a definite chief aim in life is "I just haven't had time to get around to it." An efficient leader is not necessarily the person who appears to be the busiest, but the one who can efficiently direct and keep large numbers of other people busy. The person who can "get things done" is much more profitable to a business than the one who actually does the work.

There is a mistaken notion that a person is paid for what he or she knows. This is only partly true, and like all other half-truths, it does more damage than an out-and-out falsehood. The truth is that people are paid not only for what they know, but even more for what they do with what they know, or what they can get others to do.

LEADERS DELEGATE RESPONSIBILITY

If you are a real leader, you not only have self-reliance and courage, but you impart these qualities to your subordinates. When publisher Cyrus H. K. Curtis placed a person in charge of one of his publications, he said, "I am turning this property over to you to be managed and run just exactly as if you had the legal title to it. Make your own decisions, select your own help, create your own policy, lay out your own plans, and then accept the entire responsibility for its success. All I wish to see is a satisfactory balance sheet at the end of the year."

Cyrus Curtis was one of the most successful publishers in the world. He was successful because he himself was a great leader and his leadership was based primarily on his understanding of the principle of delegating responsibility to others. He would not permit his subordinates to shift any responsibility back to him. In this way he created efficient leaders.

You will always do your best work when you feel that you are acting on your own initiative and know that you must assume full responsibility for your actions.

LEADERS SHOW THEIR INITIATIVE

[The following is adapted from How to Sell Your Way Through Life *combined with material from* Law of Success, *Volume II, Lesson Five.]*

The only way to get happiness is by giving it away to others. The same applies to the development of initiative. It is a well-known fact that one learns best what they endeavor to teach others.

In the field of salesmanship it is also a well-known fact that no salesperson is successful in selling others until they have first done a good job of selling themself.

Any statement that a person repeats over and over again for the purpose of inducing others to believe it, that person will also come to believe.

You can now see the advantage of making it your business to talk initiative, think initiative, eat initiative, sleep initiative, and practice initiative. By so doing, you become a person of initiative and leadership. People will readily, willingly, and voluntarily follow someone who shows by their actions that he or she is a person of initiative.

You should make it your business to interest others who will listen to you, in the development of initiative. It is not necessary for you to give your reasons for doing this, nor will it be necessary for you to announce that you are doing it. Just go ahead and do it. In your own mind you will understand, of course, that you are doing it because this practice will help you.

Pick out any acquaintance whom you know to be a person who never does anything that he or she is not expected to do, and begin selling them your idea of initiative. Do not stop by merely discussing the subject once; keep it up every time you have a convenient opportunity. Approach the subject from a different angle each time. If you go about this in a tactful and forceful manner, you will soon observe a change in the person. And you will observe something else of more importance: You will observe a change in yourself! You cannot talk initiative to others without developing a desire to practice it yourself.

Through the principle of autosuggestion, every statement that you make to others leaves its imprint on your own subconscious mind. If you help others develop the habit of initiative, you, in turn, develop this same habit yourself.

LEADERS MOTIVATE AND INSPIRE

[The following is adapted from **Law of Success**, Volume I, Lesson One.]

I once helped conduct a school of salesmanship for Harrison Parker, founder of the Cooperative Society of Chicago. Shortly after I started, it became apparent that the average person who joined this school would reach the top of his or her selling power within about one week. After that, these new salespeople would begin to lose their motivation and confidence, and it was necessary to revitalize the individual's enthusiasm through a group sales meeting.

Fading enthusiasm should be expected, and that is exactly why most successful sales organizations have regular sales meetings, conventions, and conferences. That is also why they actively encourage their sales people to attend seminars, read books, and listen to programs by motivational authors and speakers. The brain of a human being may be compared to an electric battery in that it will become exhausted or run down. The human brain, when in this depleted condition, must be recharged, and the manner in which this is done is through contact with a more vital mind or minds.

The weekly sales meetings I conducted for Harrison Parker were patterned after the religious revival meetings that were popular at the time. I used much the same sort of stage equipment, including music and high-powered motivational speakers who knew how to hit the right emotional buttons that would literally bring the salespeople to their feet. Whether it comes under the banner of religion, psychology, mind chemistry, or anything you please (they are all based on the same principle), by using the revival-meeting techniques I was able to motivate a group of three thousand men and women (all of whom were without former sales experience) so that they sold more than $10 million worth of securities and earned more than $1 million for themselves.

Every sales manager who is a successful leader understands the necessity of creating an esprit de corps—a spirit of common understanding and cooperation—among all the members of a sales team. That is, the salespeople as a group become so motivated and focused on a common desire, cause, or goal that the individual minds blend together and function as one.

Every leader has a method of coordinating the minds of his or her followers. One might use force; another persuasion. One will play upon the fear of penalties while another plays upon rewards. The most successful leaders in business and industry are those who get people to join and work with them because they are convinced that it is to their advantage.

If you really know how to lead, you don't rely upon your authority or power over others, nor do you try to instill fear in their hearts. You use persuasion, not power. You rely upon your ability to sell your followers by presenting the advantages to them.

MAKE YOURSELF INDISPENSABLE

[The following is adapted from material in **Law of Success**, *Volume II, Lesson Five.]*

Regardless of what you are now doing, every day brings you a chance to render some service, outside of the course of your regular duties, that will be of value to others. In rendering this additional service of your own accord, you of course understand that you are not doing so with the objective of receiving monetary pay. You are rendering this service because it provides you with ways and means of exercising, developing, and making stronger the aggressive spirit of initiative—a quality which you must possess before you can ever become an outstanding figure in your chosen field.

I employ a woman who opens, sorts, and answers much of my personal mail. She began in my employ more than three years ago. At that time her duties were to take dictation. Her salary was about the same as what others receive for similar service. One day I dictated the following motto which I asked her to type for me:

"Remember that your only limitation is the one that you set up in your own mind."

As she handed the page back to me she said, "Your motto has given me an idea that is going to be of value to both you and me."

I told her I was glad to have been of service to her. The incident made no particular impression on my mind, but from that day on I could see that it had made a tremendous impression on her mind. She began to come back to the office after supper and perform service that she was neither paid for nor expected to do. Without anyone telling her to do it, she would bring to my desk letters that she had answered for me. She had studied my style and these letters were written as well as I could have done it; in some instances even better. She kept up this habit until my personal secretary resigned. When I began to look for someone to take his place, what was more natural than to turn to this young woman. Before I had time to give her the position, she took it on her own initiative. My personal mail began to come to my desk with a new secretary's name attached, and she was that secretary. On her own time, after hours and without additional pay, she had prepared herself for the best position on my staff.

But that is not all. She soon became so noticeably efficient that she began to attract the attention of others who offered her attractive positions. I have increased her salary many times and she now receives four times what she earned when she first went to work for me as a stenographer. And, to tell you the truth, I am helpless in the matter, because she has made herself so valuable to me that I cannot get along without her.

That is initiative transformed into practical, understandable terms. I must also point out an advantage, other than a greatly increased salary, that this young lady's initiative has brought her. It has developed in her a spirit of cheerfulness that brings her happiness most stenographers never know. Her work is not work—it is a great interesting game at which she is playing. Even though she arrives at the office ahead of any of the other stenographers, and remains there long after they have watched the clock tick off five o'clock and quitting time, her hours are shorter by far than are those of the other workers. Hours of labor do not drag on the hands of those who are happy at their work.

Those who work for money alone, and who receive as their pay nothing but money, are always underpaid, no matter how much they receive. Money is of course necessary, but the big prizes of life cannot be measured in dollars and cents.

No amount of money could possibly be made to take the place of the happiness and joy and pride that belong to the person who digs a better ditch, sweeps a cleaner floor, or cooks a better meal. Every normal person loves to create something that is better than the average. The joy of creating a work of art is a joy that cannot be replaced by money or any other form of material possession.

LEADERS INSPIRE INITIATIVE IN OTHERS

[The following resumes the adapted material from **How to Sell Your Way Through Life.***]*

We do well that which we love to do, and fortunate is the leader who has the good judgment to assign all of their followers the roles that harmonize with this law.

Regardless of who you are, or what your definite chief aim may be, if you plan to attain the object of your chief aim through the cooperative efforts of others, you must set up in the minds of those whose cooperation you seek a motive strong enough to ensure their full, undivided, unselfish cooperation. When you do, you will be empowering your plans with the law of the Master Mind.

EDITOR'S NOTE

The following segment is excerpted and adapted from **Law of Success,** *Volume II, Lesson Five.*

Eighteen years ago I made my first trip to the little town of Lumberport, West Virginia. At that time the only means of transportation leading from Clarksburg, the largest nearby center, to Lumberport was either the Baltimore & Ohio Railroad or an interurban electric line which ran within three miles of the town. If you chose the trolley it meant you had to arrange for someone to pick you up or you'd have to walk the three miles to town.

Upon my arrival at Clarksburg I found that the only train going to Lumberport before noon had already gone, and not wishing to wait for the later afternoon train, I made the trip by trolley, with the intention of walking the three miles. On the way down, the rain began to pour, and those three miles had to be navigated on foot through deep yellow mud. When I arrived at Lumberport my shoes and pants were muddy and my disposition was none the better for the experience.

The first person I met was V. L. Hornor, who was then cashier of the Lumberport Bank. In a rather loud tone of voice I asked of him, "Why do you not get the trolley line extended from the junction over to Lumberport so that your friends can get in and out of town without drowning in mud?"

"Did you see a river with high banks, at the edge of town, as you came in?" he asked. I replied that I had seen it. "Well," he continued, "that's the reason we have no streetcars running into town. The cost of a bridge would be about $100,000 and that is more than the company owning the trolley line is willing to invest. We have been trying for ten years to get them to build a line into town."

"Trying?" I queried. "How hard have you tried?"

"We have offered them every inducement we could afford, such as free right of way from the junction into the town, and free use of the streets, but that bridge is the stumbling block. They simply will not pay the expense. Claim they cannot afford such an expense for the small amount of revenue they would receive from the three-mile extension."

Right then the principles of success began to come to my rescue. I asked Mr. Hornor if he would take a walk over to the river with me, that we might look at the spot that was causing so much inconvenience. He said he would be glad to do so.

When we got to the river I began to take inventory of everything in sight. I observed that the Baltimore & Ohio Railroad tracks ran up and down the river banks, on both sides of the river, and that the county road crossed the river on a rickety wooden bridge, both approaches to which had to cross over several railroad tracks because the railroad company had its switching yards at that point.

While we were standing there, a freight train blocked the road to the bridge and several teams of horses stopped on both sides of the train, waiting for an opportunity to get through. The train kept the road blocked for about twenty-five minutes.

With this combination of circumstances in mind, it required little imagination to see that three different parties could be interested in the building of the bridge such as would be needed to carry the weight of a streetcar.

It was obvious that the Baltimore & Ohio Railroad Company would be interested in such a bridge, because that would remove the county road from their switching tracks. It could also save them a possible accident on the crossing, to say nothing of much loss of time and expense in cutting trains to allow the wagon teams to pass.

It was obvious that the County Commissioners would be interested in the bridge, because it would raise the county road to a better level and make it more serviceable to the public. And of course the street railway company was interested in the bridge, but it did not wish to pay the entire cost.

All of this passed through my mind as I stood there watching the freight train being cut for the traffic to pass through.

A definite chief aim took place in my mind. Also a definite plan for its attainment. The next day I got together a committee of towns-people, consisting of the mayor, councilmen, and some of the leading citizens, and called on the Division Superintendent of the Baltimore & Ohio Railroad Company at Grafton. We convinced him that it was worth one-third of the cost of the bridge to get the county road off his company's tracks.

Next we went to the County Commissioners and found them to be quite enthusiastic over the possibility of getting a new bridge by paying for only one-third of it. They promised to pay their one-third providing we could make arrangements for the other two-thirds.

We then went to the president of the Traction Company that owned the trolley line at Fairmont, and made him an offer to donate all the rights of way and pay for two-thirds of the cost of the bridge, providing he would begin building the line into town promptly. We found him receptive also.

Three weeks later a contract had been signed between the Baltimore & Ohio Railroad Company, the Monongahela Valley Traction Company, and the County Commissioners of Harrison County, providing for the construction of the bridge—one-third of its cost to be paid by each.

Just two months later, the right of way was being graded and the bridge was under way. And three months after that, the streetcars were running into Lumberport on regular schedule.

This incident meant much to the town of Lumberport, because it provided transportation that enabled people to get in and out of the town without undue effort.

It also meant a great deal to me, because it served to introduce me as one who "got things done."

Two definite advantages resulted from this transaction. The Chief Counsel for the Traction Company gave me a position as his assistant, and later on it was the means of an introduction that led to my appointment as the advertising manager of the LaSalle Extension University.

Lumberport, West Virginia, was then and still is a small town, and Chicago was a large city and located a considerable distance away, but news of initiative and leadership has a way of taking on wings and traveling.

Although initiative and leadership were the two key elements of my success, there were actually five of the principles of success that combined in the transaction I have described here: a definite chief aim, self-confidence, imagination, initiative, and leadership. Going the extra mile, or doing more than paid for, also entered, somewhat, into this transaction, because I was not offered anything and, in fact, did not expect pay for what I did.

To be perfectly frank, I appointed myself to that job of getting the bridge built more as a sort of challenge to those who had said it could not be done than I did with the expectation of getting paid for it.

It would be helpful here to take note of the part that imagination played in this transaction. For ten years the townspeople of Lumberport had been trying to get a streetcar line built into town. It must not be concluded that the town was without any citizens of ability, because that would be inaccurate. In fact there were many able people in the town, but they had been making the mistake of trying to solve their problem through one single source, whereas there were actually three sources of solution available to them.

One hundred thousand dollars was too much for one company to assume for the construction of a bridge, but when the cost was divided among three interested parties, the amount to be borne by each was more reasonable. The question might be asked, why did some of the local townspeople not think of this three-way solution?

In the first place, they were so close to the problem that they failed to see it from a perspective which would have suggested the solution. This is a common mistake and one that is always avoided by great leaders.

In the second place, these townspeople had never before coordinated their efforts or worked as an organized group with the sole purpose in mind of finding a way to get a streetcar line built into town. This is another common error made by people in all walks of life—that of failure to work in unison, in a thorough spirit of cooperation.

I, being an outsider, had less difficulty in getting cooperative action than one of their own group might have had. Too often there is a spirit of selfishness in small communities that prompts each individual to think that their ideas should prevail. It is an important part of the leader's responsibility to induce people to subordinate their own ideas and interests for the good of the project or goal.

Success is nearly always a question of your ability to get others to subordinate their own individual interests and follow a leader. The person who has the initiative, personality, and the imagination to induce followers to accept his or her plans and carry them out faithfully is always an able leader.

Leadership, initiative, and imagination are so closely allied and so essential for success that one cannot be gainfully applied without the other. Initiative is the moving force that pushes the leader ahead, but imagination is the guiding spirit that tells him or her which way to go.

Imagination is what enabled me to analyze the Lumberport bridge problem, break it up into its three component parts, and then assemble those parts into a practical working plan. Nearly every problem may be broken up into parts that are more easily managed, as parts, than they are when assembled as a whole. Perhaps one of the most important advantages of imagination is that it enables you to separate all problems into their component parts and to reassemble them into more favorable combinations.

It has been said that all battles in warfare are won or lost not on the firing line but behind the lines, through the sound strategy, or the lack of it, used by the generals who plan the battles.

This is equally true in business and in most other problems that confront us throughout life. We win or lose according to the nature of the plans we build and carry out.

There is no escape from this truth. Organized effort is effort that is directed according to a plan that is conceived with the aid of imagination, guided by a definite chief aim, and given momentum with self-confidence and initiative. These principles of success blend into one and become a power in the hands of a leader. Without the blending of these principles, and the initiative to pull them together and make use of them, effective leadership is impossible.

Chapter II

PERSISTENCE

———————

I would like to call your attention to a principle that I believe to be the factor, more than any other, which determines whether one succeeds or fails in any calling. The principle may be described as "the faith and persistence to accept defeat as being nothing more than an experience from which something of value may be learned." Most people give up or let their ambition be killed when serious obstacles are met.

It has been my privilege during my public career to know many men and women of great achievement. And all of them had met with opposition that necessitated struggle and persistence. Life is filled with obstacles that must be overcome. Only those who have the stamina and the willingness to fight can win. Everyone meets with opposition. Opposition should be accepted as a signal to put everything you have into its mastery.

When defeat comes, as it will, accept it as a hurdle that has been placed in your way for the purpose of training you to jump higher! You will gain strength and skill from each hurdle that you surmount. Do not hate people because they oppose you. Thank them for forcing you to develop the strategy and imagination you will need to master their opposition.

This is a beautiful world and life is stocked with an abundance of everything you need, including riches and happiness.

Accept both the bitter and the sweet. Success without defeat would lead to boredom. Defeat without the counteracting effect of success would kill ambition. Be willing to accept your portion of each.

Every failure will teach you a lesson that you need to learn if you will keep your eyes and ears open and be willing to be taught. Every adversity is usually a blessing in disguise. Without reverses and temporary defeat, you would never know just how good you are.

THREE FEET FROM GOLD

[This section on persistence is excerpted from **Think and Grow Rich: The 21st-Century Edition.***]*

One of the most common causes of failure is the habit of quitting when you are overtaken by temporary defeat. Every person is guilty of this mistake at one time or another.

During the gold-rush days, an uncle of R. U. Darby was caught by "gold fever" and he went west to Colorado to dig and grow rich. He had never heard that more gold has been mined from the thoughts of men than has ever been taken from the earth. He staked a claim and went to work with pick and shovel.

After weeks of labor, he was rewarded with the discovery of the shining ore. But he needed machinery to bring the ore to the surface. Quietly he covered up the mine and returned to his home in Williamsburg, Maryland. He told his relatives and a few neighbors about the strike. They got together the money for the machinery and then had it shipped. My friend R. U. Darby decided to join his uncle and they went back to work the mine.

The first car of ore was mined and shipped to a smelter. The returns proved they had one of the richest mines in Colorado. A few more cars of ore would clear their debts. Then would come the big killing in profits.

Down went the drills. Up went the hopes of Darby and uncle. Then something happened. The vein of gold ore disappeared! They had come to the end of the rainbow, and the pot of gold was no longer there. They drilled on, desperately trying to pick up the vein again—all to no avail. Finally, they decided to quit.

They sold the machinery to a junkman for a few hundred dollars and took the train back home. The junkman called in a mining engineer to look at the mine and do a little calculating. The engineer advised that the project had failed because the owners were not familiar with "fault lines." His calculations showed that the vein would be found just three feet from where the Darbys had stopped drilling. And that is exactly where it was found!

The junkman took millions of dollars in ore from the mine because he knew enough to seek expert counsel before giving up.

Long afterward, Mr. Darby recouped his loss many times over when he made the discovery that desire can be transmuted into gold. The discovery came after he went into the business of selling life insurance.

Never forgetting that he lost a huge fortune because he stopped three feet from gold, Darby profited by the experience in his newly chosen field. He said to himself, "I stopped three feet from gold, but I will never stop because men say no when I ask them to buy insurance."

He became one of a small group who sell over a million dollars in life insurance annually. He owed his "stickability" to the lesson he learned from his "quitability" in the gold-mining business.

Shortly after Mr. Darby received his degree from the "University of Hard Knocks," he witnessed something that proved to him that no does not necessarily mean NO.

One afternoon he was helping his uncle grind wheat in an old-fashioned mill. The uncle operated a large farm on which a number of sharecropper farmers lived. Quietly the door opened and a small child, the daughter of a tenant, walked in and took her place near the door.

The uncle looked up, saw the child, and barked at her roughly, "What do you want?"

Meekly, the child replied, "My mom says to send her fifty cents."

"I'll not do it," the uncle retorted. "Now you run on home."

But she did not move. The uncle went ahead with his work, not noticing that she did not leave. When he looked up again and saw her still standing there, he said, "I told you to go on home! Now go, or I'll take a switch to you."

She did not budge. The uncle dropped a sack of grain he was about to pour into the mill hopper, and started toward the child.

Darby held his breath. He knew his uncle had a fierce temper.

When the uncle reached the spot where the child was standing, she quickly came forward one step, looked up into his eyes, and screamed at the top of her voice, "My mom's gotta have that fifty cents!"

The uncle stopped, looked at her for a minute, put his hand in his pocket, took out half a dollar, and gave it to her.

The child took the money and slowly backed toward the door, never taking her eyes off the man whom she had just conquered. After she had gone, the uncle sat down on a box and looked out the window into space for more than ten minutes. He was pondering, with awe, over the whipping he had just taken.

Mr. Darby was also doing some thinking. That was the first time in all his experience that he had seen a child deliberately master an adult. How did she do it? What happened to his uncle that caused him to lose his fierceness and become as docile as a lamb? What strange power did this child use that made her master of the situation?

Strangely, the story of this unusual experience was told to me in the old mill, on the very spot where the uncle took his whipping. As we stood there in that musty old mill, Mr. Darby repeated the story, and finished by asking, "What can you make of it? What strange power did that child use that so completely whipped my uncle?"

Then he mentally retraced his thirty years as a life insurance salesman. As he did so, it became clear that his success was due, in no small degree, to the lesson he had learned from that child.

Mr. Darby pointed out: "Every time a prospect tried to bow me out, without buying, I saw that child standing there in the old mill, her big eyes glaring in defiance, and I said to myself: 'I've got to make this sale.' The better portion of all sales I have made were made after people had said no."

Before success comes in anyone's life, that person is sure to meet with much temporary defeat and, perhaps, some failure. When defeat overtakes a person, the easiest and most logical thing to do is to quit. That is exactly what the majority of people do.

More than five hundred of the most successful people this country has ever known told me their greatest success came just one step beyond the point at which defeat had overtaken them. Failure is a trickster with a keen sense of irony and cunning. It takes great delight in tripping you just when success is almost within reach.

EDITOR'S NOTE

Napoleon Hill's creed, "Every failure brings with it the seed of an equivalent success," was the inspiration for entrepreneur and motivational speaker Wayne Allyn Root to write his book **The Joy of Failure**. *Published in the late 1990s, it not only tells Wayne's personal story of using his failures as steppingstones to success, but he also recounts stories from other successful people which prove that the rich and famous only got to be rich and famous because of what they learned from their failures. People such as Jack Welch, the hugely successful CEO of General Electric, who, early in his career failed dramatically when a plastics plant for which he was responsible blew up. Billionaire Charles Schwab was a failure at school and university, flunking Basic English twice due to a learning disability, and then failed on Wall Street more than once, before he thought of the idea that grew to make him very rich indeed. Sylvester Stallone, Bruce Willis, Oprah Winfrey, Bill Clinton, Steven Jobs, Donald Trump, and a host of other equally well-known achievers all had to fail in order to learn the lessons that ultimately made them successes. Every one of them has been a failure, but none of them was defeated.*

Charles F. Kettering, who patented more than two hundred inventions including the automobile ignition, the spark plug, Freon for air conditioners, and the automatic transmission, said, "From the time a person is six years old until he graduates from college, he has to take three or four examinations a year. If he flunks once, he is out. But an inventor is almost always failing. He tries and fails maybe a thousand times. If he succeeds once, then he's in. These two things are diametrically opposite. We often say that the biggest job we have is to teach a newly hired employee how to fail intelligently. We have to train him to experiment over and over and to keep on trying and failing until he learns what will work. Failures are just practice shots."

The following segment is adapted in part from a transcription of the video program **The Master Key to Success** *and from the Napoleon Hill Foundation's publication* **Believe and Achieve.**

One of the best examples of finding the seed of an equivalent benefit in failure is the story of a man of whom you may have heard, and I have no doubt that you've eaten some of the food he produced and marketed throughout the nation as the result of an adversity which would have stopped most men cold.

The man was Milo C. Jones, who owned a farm near Fort Atkinson, Wisconsin. Although he was a hard worker and his physical health was good, he seemed unable to make his small farm yield more than the bare necessities of life. Then he suffered a stroke and was stricken down with double paralysis, which deprived him of the use of every portion of his body except his brain. He was put to bed by his relatives who believed him to be a helpless invalid.

For weeks he remained unable to move a single muscle. All he had left was his mind, the one great power he had drawn upon so rarely because he had earned his living by the use of his brawn. Out of this sheer necessity he discovered the power of his mind and began to draw upon it.

Jones called his family together and told them: "I can no longer work with my hands, so I have decided to work with my mind. The rest of you will have to take the place of my hands." In this hour of his greatest adversity, Milo C. Jones used his mind—took possession of it for the first time in his life, perhaps—and out of that mind came the idea that would yield him a huge fortune.

He told his assembled family that this year they were going to start planting every acre of the farm they could spare in corn, then start raising pigs with that corn; slaughter the pigs while they are young and tender, and convert them into sausage.

The family went to work, and in a few years the trade name of Jones Little Pig Sausages became a household byword throughout the nation. Jones was the first to raise hogs specifically for producing premium sausage; prior to this innovation, sausage had always been thought of as a byproduct. The Jones company was also the first in its field to rely heavily on mail-order sales and on an aggressive national advertising program to promote its products.

Milo C. Jones lived to see himself earn a multimillion dollar fortune from the same farm which previous to his misfortune had yielded him only a scant living.

Isn't it strange that so often people have to be cut down by failure and defeat before they learn they have minds capable of mastering all of their problems? Isn't it strange that Jones did not discover the Little Pig Sausage idea while he had a sound body?

TAKE YOUR OWN PERSISTENCE INVENTORY

Persistence is a state of mind, therefore it can be cultivated. Like all states of mind, persistence is based upon definite causes, among them these:

1. *Definiteness of purpose.* Knowing what you want is the first and most important step toward the development of persistence. A strong motive will force you to surmount difficulties.

2. *Desire.* It is comparatively easy to acquire and maintain persistence in pursuing the object of intense desire.

3. *Self-reliance.* Belief in your ability to carry out a plan encourages you to follow the plan through with persistence. (Self-reliance can be developed through the principle described in the chapter on autosuggestion.)

4. *Definiteness of plans.* Organized plans, even ones that may be weak or impractical, encourage persistence.

5. *Accurate knowledge.* Knowing that your plans are sound, based upon experience or observation, encourages persistence; "guessing" instead of "knowing" destroys persistence.

6. *Cooperation.* Sympathy, understanding, and cooperation with others tend to develop persistence.

7. *Willpower.* The habit of concentrating your thoughts on making plans to attain your definite purpose leads to persistence.

8. *Habit.* Persistence is the direct result of habit. The mind absorbs and becomes a part of the daily experiences upon which it feeds. Fear, the worst of all enemies, can be overcome by forcing yourself to perform and repeat acts of courage.

Take inventory of yourself and determine what you are lacking in this essential quality of persistence. Measure yourself, point by point, and see how many of the previous eight factors of persistence you lack. This analysis may lead to discoveries that will give you a new understanding of yourself and what you need to get ahead.

BAD HABITS TO OVERCOME

The following is a list of the real enemies that stand between you and achievement. These are not only the "symptoms" indicating weakness of persistence, but also the deeply seated subconscious causes of this weakness. Study the list carefully, and face yourself squarely if you really wish to know who you are and what you are capable of doing. These are the weaknesses that must be mastered by anyone who really wants to accumulate riches:

1.   Failure to recognize and to define clearly exactly what you want.

2.   Procrastination, with or without cause. (Usually backed up with a long list of alibis and excuses.)

3.   Lack of interest in acquiring specialized knowledge.

4.   Indecision, and the habit of passing the buck instead of facing issues squarely. (Also backed by alibis and excuses.)

5.   The habit of relying upon excuses instead of making definite plans to solve your problems.

6.   Self-satisfaction, for which there is little remedy and no hope for those who suffer from it.

7.   Indifference, usually reflected in your readiness to compromise rather than meet opposition and fight it.

8.   The habit of blaming others for your mistakes, and accepting circumstances as being unavoidable.

9.   Weakness of desire because you neglected to choose motives that will push you to take action.

10. Willingness to quit at the first sign of defeat. (Based upon one or more of the six basic fears.)

11. Lack of organized plans you have written out so they can be analyzed.

12. The habit of neglecting to act on ideas, or to grasp opportunity when it presents itself.

13. Wishing instead of willing.

14. The habit of compromising with poverty instead of aiming at riches. A general lack of ambition to be, to do, or to own.

15. Searching for all the shortcuts to riches, trying to get without giving a fair equivalent. Usually reflected in the habit of gambling, or trying to drive unfair bargains.

16. Fear of criticism, resulting in failure to create plans and put them into action, because of what other people might think, do, or say. This is one of your most dangerous enemies, because it often exists in your subconscious mind and you may not even know it is there.

THE FEAR OF CRITICISM

The majority of people permit relatives, friends, and the public at large to influence them so that they cannot live their own lives because they fear criticism.

Many people make mistakes in marriage but stay married, because they fear criticism. Millions of people neglect to go back and get an education after having left school, because they fear criticism. Countless numbers of men and women permit relatives to wreck their lives in the name of family duty, because they fear criticism.

People refuse to take chances in business, because they fear the criticism that may follow if they fail. The fear of criticism in such cases is stronger than the desire for success.

Too many people refuse to set high goals for themselves, because they fear the criticism of relatives and friends who may say, "Don't aim so high. People will think you are crazy."

When Andrew Carnegie suggested that I devote twenty years to the organization of a philosophy of individual achievement, my first impulse was fear of what people might say. His suggestion was far greater than anything I had ever conceived for myself. My first instinct was to create excuses, all of them traceable to the fear of criticism. Something inside of me said, "You can't do it. The job is too big and requires too much time. What will your relatives think of you? How will you earn a living? No one has ever organized a philosophy of success, what right have you to believe you can do it? Who are you, anyway, to aim so high? Remember your humble birth—what do you know about philosophy? People will think you are crazy (and they did). Why hasn't some other person done this before now?"

Later in life, after having analyzed thousands of people, I discovered that most ideas are stillborn. To grow, ideas need the breath of life injected into them through definite plans of immediate action. The time to nurse an idea is at the time of its birth. Every minute it lives gives it a better chance of surviving. The fear of criticism is what kills most ideas that never reach the planning and action stage.

THE HABIT OF DOING MORE THAN PAID FOR

[The following is adapted from material in **Law of Success**, *Volume III, Lesson Nine.]*

A few years ago I was invited to deliver the graduation address before the students of a college. During my address I dwelt at length, and with all the emphasis at my command, on the importance of rendering more service and better service than that for which one is paid.

After the address was delivered, the president and the secretary of the college invited me to join them for lunch. While we were eating, the secretary turned to the president and said, "I have just found out what this man is doing. He is putting himself ahead in the world by first helping others to get ahead."

In that brief statement he had epitomized one of the most important parts of my philosophy on the subject of success: It is literally true that you can succeed best and quickest by helping others to succeed.

Some years ago, when I was in the advertising business, I built my entire clientele by applying the fundamentals upon which this lesson is founded. By having my name placed on the lists of various mail-order houses, I received their sales literature. When I received a sales letter or a booklet or a folder that I believed I could improve, I went right to work and made the improvements, then sent it back to the firm that had sent it to me, with a letter stating that this was but a trifling sample of what I could do—that there were plenty of other good ideas where that one came from—and that I would be glad to render regular service for a monthly fee.

Invariably this brought an order for my services. Even on the one occasion when a firm was dishonest enough to appropriate my idea and use it without paying me for it, it still turned out to be an advantage to me. A member of the firm who was familiar with the situation started another business, and as a result of the work I had done for his former associates, for which I was not paid, he hired me at more than double the amount I would have realized from his original firm.

EDITOR'S NOTE

It was Napoleon Hill's position that if a person performs no more service than that for which the person is being paid, then obviously that person is receiving all the pay that he or she deserves. The following example, adapted from one of Hill's recorded lectures, is one of his favorite stories to illustrate this point.

When Charles M. Schwab first came to Andrew Carnegie's attention, Schwab was working as a day laborer in one of Carnegie's steel plants. Mr. Carnegie observed that Mr. Schwab always performed more and better service than that for which he was paid. Moreover, he performed it with a pleasing attitude which made him popular among his fellow workers.

Mr. Schwab was promoted from one job to another until he was finally made president of the great United States Steel Corporation, at a salary of $75,000 a year. What's more, on some occasions Mr. Carnegie not only paid Mr. Schwab's salary, but he also gave him a bonus of as much as one million dollars.

Think of it. Charles M. Schwab the day laborer could never have earned that much in his entire lifetime—a salary of $75,000 a year paid to a man who started as a day laborer, plus a bonus of more than ten times that amount! Why do you suppose Mr. Carnegie paid him that much?

When asked, Mr. Carnegie said, "I gave him his salary for the work he actually performed, and the bonus for his willingness to go the extra mile, thus setting a fine example for his fellow workers."

EDITOR'S NOTE

The following resumes from How to Sell Your Way Through Life*.*

The habit of giving more service and better service than you are paid to render is absolutely essential to the marketing of yourself and your personal services. Among the many sound reasons for rendering more service and better service than expected are the following:

1. This habit turns the spotlight of favorable attention upon those who develop it.

2. This habit enables you to profit by the law of contrast, since the majority of people have formed the habit of offering as little service as they can get away with.

3. This habit gives you the benefit of the law of increasing returns and ensures against the disadvantages of the law of decreasing returns, eventually enabling you to receive more pay than you would receive without this habit.

4. This habit ensures you preferred employment at preferred wages. The person who practices this habit is the last to be removed from the payroll when business is poor and the first to be taken back after a layoff.

5. This habit develops greater skill, efficiency, and also greater earning ability, and it tends to give you preference over others.

6. This habit makes you practically indispensable and will prompt your employer to delegate greater responsibilities to you. The capacity to assume responsibility is the quality that brings the highest monetary returns.

7. This habit leads to promotion because it indicates that those who practice it have ability for supervision and leadership not found in those who follow the opposite habit.

8. This habit enables you to set your own salary. If you can't get as much as you deserve from one employer, it may be obtained from the competitors.

Every business has either a potential or a real asset known as goodwill. It is an asset without which no business can grow. An individual who renders more service and better service than paid for may also be said to have this goodwill asset. It is generally known as your reputation for efficiency. It is an asset without which you cannot market your personal services to best advantage.

The strongest and most attractive selling feature any individual has is the habit of rendering service that is greater in quantity and superior in quality.

The habit of rendering more service and better service works in behalf of an employer just as it does in behalf of an employee.

Every individual who works for a salary naturally wants more money and a better position. Not every such individual, however, understands that better positions and greater pay come as the result of motive, and that the greatest of all motives with which these desirable benefits may be attracted is that of rendering more service and better service than one is paid to render.

You are a merchant and your ability is the product you sell. Use the same principles of sound judgment in marketing yourself that a successful merchant uses in marketing products. You know, of course, what happens if you are a merchant who shortchanges the customers; you lose their business. On the other hand, you also know what happens to the merchant who builds confidence by rendering service and delivering merchandise that meets the customer's expectations.

Most people can cheat others occasionally without detection. But you can't cheat others without observation by your own conscience. Your conscience is the official recorder of your acts and thoughts, and it writes the record of every thought and deed into the fabric of your character.

A clear conscience is an asset comparable to no other, especially when you are selling yourself. Master salesmanship, regardless of the wares you may be selling, is based upon absolute faith in the thing you are offering for sale. How can you believe in yourself if you know that you have cheated?

EDITOR'S NOTE

The following is excerpted and adapted from **Law of Success,** *Volume III, Lesson Nine.*

Ralph Waldo Emerson wrote in his essay Compensation:

. . . The law of Nature is, Do the thing and you shall have the power; but they who do not the thing have not the power. . . .

. . . Men suffer all their life long, under the foolish superstition that they can be cheated. But it is as impossible for a man to be cheated by anyone but himself, as for a thing to be, and not to be, at the same time. . . .

EDITOR'S NOTE

If you are interested in reading Ralph Waldo Emerson's Compensation online you can find it at:

http://www.rwe.org/works/Essays-1st_Series_03_Compensation.htm.

We go through two important periods in life. One is that period during which we are gathering, classifying, and organizing knowledge, and the other is that period during which we are struggling for recognition.

One of the most important reasons why we should always be not only ready but also willing to render service is that every time we do so, we gain an opportunity to prove to someone that we have ability. We go just one more step toward gaining the necessary recognition that we must all have.

Instead of saying to the world, "Show me the color of your money and I will show you what I can do," reverse it and say, "Let me show you the color of my service so that I may take a look at the color of your money if you like my service."

Here is a perfect example that involves a woman who was working as a stenographer at fifteen dollars a week. Judging by the salary, she must have been none too competent in that work.

About ten years later, this same woman was clearing a little over $100,000 on the lecture circuit. What bridged that mighty chasm between these two earning capacities? The habit of doing more than paid for. This woman became well known throughout the country as a prominent lecturer on the subject of applied psychology.

Let me show you how she harnessed the law of increasing returns. First she went into a city and delivered a series of fifteen free lectures. Anyone could attend, at no charge. As she was delivering these lectures she had the opportunity of "selling herself" to her audience, and at the end of the series she announced the formation of a class for which she charged twenty-five dollars per student.

That's all there was to her plan. While she was commanding a small fortune for a year's work, there were scores of much more proficient lecturers who were barely getting enough from their work to pay their expenses, simply because they had not yet familiarized themselves, as she had, with the fundamentals upon which this lesson is based.

If this woman lecturer, who had no extraordinary qualifications, could harness the law of increasing returns and make it raise her from the position of stenographer at fifteen dollars a week to that of lecturer at over $100,000 a year, why can you not apply this same law so that it will give you advantages you do not have now?

EDITOR'S NOTE

At a later time, Hill himself used the same principle but he combined it with the leading technology of his day. Napoleon Hill took his lecture series and turned it into radio programs, and later television shows, that were broadcast by local stations in the cities where Hill was speaking or promoting his books. These were but a more sophisticated version of "free" lectures that enticed listeners and viewers to see him for themselves and perhaps buy his books.

The Silva Method, a success system developed by Jose Silva and based on concepts very similar to those espoused by Napoleon Hill, became popular using essentially that same principle. Beginning in the late 1960s, every weekend in newspapers in most major cities in North America, advertisements would appear offering a free introductory course provided by a local trainer certified in the Silva Method. These free introductions convinced enough participants to become paying customers that the Silva Method grew into one of the most successful self-help courses of all time.

In the 1980s the principle evolved again, only this time the free lecture was called an infomercial. But in essence it was the same concept: it was a way for audiences to sample ideas and speakers. Once again the principle worked, and in the case of Anthony Robbins, for example, it launched a true phenomenon into the world of motivational speaking.

The following continues from **Law of Success**, *Volume III, Lesson Nine.*

Several years ago I was invited to deliver a lecture before the students of the Palmer School in Davenport, Iowa. My manager completed arrangements for me to accept the invitation under the regular terms in effect at that time, which were $100 for the lecture plus my travel expenses.

When I arrived in Davenport I found a reception committee awaiting me at the depot, and that evening I was given one of the warmest welcomes I had ever received during my public career, up to that time. I met many delightful people from whom I gathered many valuable facts that were of benefit to me. Therefore, when I was asked to make out my expense account so the school could give me a check, I told them that I had received my pay, many times over, by what I had learned while I was there. I refused my fee and returned to my office in Chicago feeling well repaid for the trip.

The following morning Dr. Palmer went before the two thousand students of his school and announced what I had said about feeling repaid, and he added: "In the twenty years that I have been conducting this school I have had scores of speakers address the student body, but this is the first time I ever knew a man to refuse his fee because he felt that he had been repaid for his services in other ways. This man is the editor of a national magazine and I advise every one of you to subscribe to that magazine, because such a man as this must have much that each of you will need when you go into the field and offer your services."

By the middle of that week I had received more than $6,000 for subscriptions. During the following two years these same two thousand students and their friends sent in more than $50,000 for subscriptions. Tell me how or where I could have invested $100 as profitably as this.

EDITOR'S NOTE

To close this section on doing more than paid for, or going the extra mile, we have chosen one of Napoleon Hill's favorite stories about a salesman. This anecdote seems almost too good to be true, but since Hill knew the Carnegie family personally, it is unlikely he would tell the story if it were not true. This version of the tale is from **Law of Success,** *Volume III, Lesson Nine.*

One rainy afternoon an elderly lady walked into a Pittsburgh department store and wandered around in an aimless sort of way, very much in the manner that people who have no intention of buying often do. Most of the salespeople gave her the "once over" and busied themselves by straightening the stock on their shelves so as to avoid being troubled by her.

One of the young men saw her and made it his business to inquire politely if he might serve her. She informed him that she was only waiting for it to stop raining; that she did not wish to make any purchases. The young man assured her that she was welcome and, by engaging her in conversation, made her feel that he had meant what he said. When she was ready to go, he accompanied her to the street and raised her umbrella for her. She asked for his card and went on her way.

The incident had been forgotten by the young man, when one day he was called into the office by the head of the firm and shown a letter from a lady who wanted a salesman to go to Scotland and take an order for the furnishings for a mansion.

That lady was Andrew Carnegie's mother; she was also the same woman whom the young man had so courteously escorted to the street many months previously.

In the letter, Mrs. Carnegie specified that this young man was the one whom she desired to be sent to take her order. The order amounted to an enormous sum, and this incident brought the young man an opportunity for advancement that he might never have had except for his courtesy to an elderly lady who did not look like a "ready sale."

Just as the great fundamental laws of life are wrapped up in the commonest sort of everyday experiences that most of us never notice, so are the real opportunities often hidden in the seemingly unimportant transactions of life.

Chapter 12

MAKING THE SALE

EDITOR'S NOTE

The following is from **How to Sell Your Way Through Life**.

In the actual process of selling, the first step is to qualify the prospective buyer. That is, the salesperson must find out the following information that will be needed in presenting the sales plan to the best advantage. The salesperson will probably have to find ways to tactfully get this information from the prospective buyer as well as from other sources.

QUALIFYING THE PROSPECTIVE BUYER

1. How much money is the prospective buyer prepared to spend and how much should the buyer be asked to spend?

2. Are conditions, including the prospective buyer's state of mind, favorable for closing the sale? If not, when are they likely to be?

3. Will the prospective buyer act alone or must some lawyer, banker, spouse, relative, counselor, or other person be consulted before a decision can be reached? If so, who is the person to be consulted and for what specific purpose?

4. If the prospective buyer must consult another person before making a decision, will the buyer permit the salesperson to be present at the consultation? This is highly important. You can't afford for a third person to sit in judgment of you and your wares without being there to present your own case.

5. Does the prospective buyer like to do most of the talking? If so, be sure to give them the opportunity. Every word that a prospective buyer speaks will serve as a clue to what is in the buyer's mind. If the prospective buyer is not inclined to talk freely, ask leading questions that will bring out the desired information.

While qualifying the prospective buyer, the salesperson will also learn what excuse or objections are likely to be offered when the closing point has been reached. The following are some of the most commonly used excuses to which practically all prospective buyers resort:

1. The prospective buyer will claim not to have the money. The master salesperson always takes this one with more than the proverbial grain of salt. If you are a sales professional, you have already accurately qualified the prospective buyer, so you know the buyer's financial status and can, therefore, tactfully meet this objection.

2. The prospective buyer may tell the salesperson that he or she does not wish to decide until he or she has talked the matter over with a spouse, banker, lawyer. The master salesperson will tactfully invite the client to permit the salesperson to talk to both the client and the client's adviser together. At this interview the master salesperson will analyze the spouse or other confidante and ascertain whether he or she is a partner, the real boss, or a mere subterfuge. Needless to say, if the spouse is the boss, the salesperson will direct the sales efforts mainly to that person.

3. The prospective buyer may claim to need more time to "think the matter over." The master salesperson knows about how much "thinking" the majority of people do. However, the salesperson

will use tact in such cases, and will suggest ways and means by which to assist the prospective buyer in the task of thinking. The master salesperson permits prospective buyers to believe they are doing their own thinking, but the sales professional takes care to see that they think with ideas and facts which the salesperson supplies.

If you are a master salesperson you never try to close a sale until you are absolutely sure that you have painted a picture in the prospective buyer's mind that has created a strong desire for your goods or services. The prospective buyer must *be able to buy.* This is a point on which no guessing should be done. It is the master salesperson's business to know, and if you do not know, you are not a master salesperson.

Trying to sell a Cadillac to a person who has a Ford bank account is wasted effort. Accurate qualification prevents such waste.

The first thing a master salesperson asks a prospective purchaser of life insurance is, "How much insurance do you now carry and what sort of policies do you have now?" Armed with this information, and knowing the prospective buyer's approximate financial status, the life insurance salesperson knows what policy to offer the client.

ENCOURAGE YOUR CUSTOMER TO TALK FREELY

When police officials are called in to solve a murder mystery the thing they want to know is the motive. Unless the motive for the crime has been established, it is often difficult to apprehend the criminal, and then to convict him after he has been apprehended. Anyone is already beaten when an adversary gains possession of the motives by which that person is inspired to action.

When police officials arrest a man who is suspected of having committed a crime, they immediately try to convince the suspect to talk. Every word uttered, as well as any refusal to talk on certain points, gives the investigators information from which they can make important deductions.

Until the actual presentation of your sales plan, you should be like one of those police investigators. It is your business to get the facts, and the best method of getting them is to get your prospective buyer to talk. Some who call themselves salespeople spoil their chances of making sales by opening their mouths and closing their eyes and ears. Find out your prospective buyer's major motives and major weaknesses, and that buyer is as good as yours before you begin.

The most successful salespeople manage their interviews so tactfully that the prospective buyers believe that they are managing it. When the sale has been closed, the buyer believes he or she has made a purchase rather than having been sold anything.

Master salespeople prepare themselves by putting together a set of stock questions they can use to get the information they will need to accurately qualify potential buyers. Care and thought in preparing and asking these questions will enable you to get all the information needed to close a sale. Most people will answer any reasonable questions they are asked. By asking the prospect directly, you will be sure the information is reliable because the prospect will supply it.

The salesperson who is too indifferent or too lazy to qualify their prospective buyers deserves to fail, and such salespeople usually do.

BUILDING BUYER CONFIDENCE

Master salespeople often make it a part of their technique to contact prospective buyers in advance of any sales call. Their first contact is simply to qualify the buyer in an unobtrusive manner. I have known many master salespeople who have entertained their prospective buyers for months while establishing confidence, meanwhile refraining from any attempt to make sales.

One of the most successful life insurance salespeople in America specializes in the sale of insurance policies to men with whom he plays golf. He takes great care, however, never to refer to his profession, even briefly, on the golf course. Moreover, he never tries to talk insurance to his prospective buyers until after he has played golf with them at least three times. Even then he leads up to the subject through well-prepared, tactful, questions which prompt his prospective buyers to ask him about insurance.

He calls himself an insurance counselor. He tells prospective buyers that his business is to go over their insurance policies with them to see whether or not they have the best form of insurance, the right amount, and so forth. Naturally, he chooses prospective buyers who carry large amounts of insurance and who, therefore, have many policies already in force. He has made hundreds of sales without asking his prospective buyers to take additional insurance, merely by analyzing their insurance schedules in such a tactful way as to plant in their minds the thought that they need additional insurance of one sort or another.

Confidence must be created by the master salesperson in the minds of prospective buyers. If you qualify your prospective buyers properly, you build their confidence while doing so.

All of this process of qualifying the prospective buyer must be done before you attempt to close the sale. Practically every sale that is lost after the sales presentation has been made occurs for one of two reasons:

First, the salesperson has failed to accurately qualify the prospective buyer before making the sales presentation.

And second, the salesperson has not properly neutralized the mind of the prospective buyer before trying to close the sale.

NEUTRALIZING THE BUYER'S MIND

After the prospective buyer has been qualified, or during the qualification process before a sale can be made, the customer's mind must be emptied of negative attitude, bias, resentment, and all other conditions unfavorable to the salesperson. The prospective buyer's mind must be cultivated and prepared before the seed of desire can be successfully planted in it.

A neutral or favorable prospective buyer has the following:

1. *Confidence:* The buyer must have confidence in the salesperson and in the goods or services.

2. *Interest:* The buyer must be reached through an appeal to his or her imagination, and through the interest it aroused in the commodity offered for sale.

3. *Motive:* The buyer must always have a logical motive for buying. The building of this motive is the salesperson's most important task.

No prospective buyer's mind has been neutralized and made favorable until these three conditions exist in their mind.

The salesperson's first duty is to create confidence in the mind of the prospective buyer. Nothing builds confidence more quickly than a genuine interest in the buyer's business problems. The smart professional salesperson makes a careful analysis of the buyer, the buyer's business, and the ups and downs the buyer has to face in doing his or her business.

The salesperson's second duty in preparing the buyer's mind is to arouse interest in the goods or services to be sold. To arouse interest in your wares, you will have to use imagination, faith, enthusiasm, knowledge of your merchandise, persistence, and showmanship. A neutral mind will be of no advantage to you if you lack the ability to plant in that mind the seed of desire for your merchandise. And that seed cannot be planted without interest on the part of the prospective buyer.

The salesperson's third duty is to create an appropriate motive to induce the prospective buyer to purchase their wares. This means you have to have full and complete knowledge of the prospective buyer and the buyer's business.

Failure to neutralize the mind of the prospective buyer is one of the five major weaknesses of unsuccessful salespeople. There is no fixed rule to be followed in neutralizing the minds of prospective buyers. Each individual case offers conditions peculiar unto itself, and each case must be handled on its own merits.

Some of the methods which have been used to neutralize are as follows:

1. *Social contacts* through sports, fitness, or recreational clubs. It has been said that more business is done on the golf courses than is done in business offices. Certainly every master salesperson knows the value of networking and club contacts.

2. *Religious affiliations.* You may make acquaintances through your church, synagogue, or mosque. Connections made in these circumstances tend to establish confidence.

3. *Business associations*, fraternities, lodges, and union affiliations. In many lines of selling, it will be very helpful for the salesperson to establish contacts through organizations based on common background or interests, where people naturally let down the bars of formality.

4. *Personal courtesies.* Dinner engagements offer favorable opportunity to establish confidence, which in turn helps to neutralize the mind.

5. *Personal service.* Under some conditions salespeople are in a position to render valuable service and to supply helpful information to those with whom they intend to do business subsequently.

6. *Mutual interests and hobbies.* Nearly everyone has a hobby or some form of interest outside of business. When discussing or pursuing a hobby or leisure interest, people are always inclined to step out from behind their usual defenses.

Having neutralized the mind of the buyer, and having established confidence, the next step in making a sale is to crystallize that confidence into interest in your goods or services. Here you must build your entire sales presentation around a central motive that is appropriate and best suited to the business and financial status of your prospective buyer. Once you have established confidence, created interest, and also appealed to motive, you have reached the point at which the sale may be closed.

THE SUCCESSFUL SALE IS LIKE A THREE-ACT PLAY

Salesmanship involves principles similar to those on which a successful stage play, movie, or television drama is based. The psychology of selling an individual is closely akin to that which is used by actors in selling an audience:

Act I, Interest: The script that succeeds must have a strong opening act that grabs the attention and arouses the interest of the audience. Interest must be created by neutralizing the mind of the prospective buyer and establishing confidence, and your approach must be strong enough to arouse interest in both the salesperson and in the goods or services. If you fall down in this first act, you will experience difficulty, if not impossibility, in making a sale.

Act II, Desire: Desire must be developed through the proper presentation of motive. Your sales presentation may be weak "in the middle" without killing the sale, providing the opening and the close are strong and impelling. The second act develops the plot, and the audience will be charitable, providing they liked the first act well enough to believe there will be a strong climax.

Act III, Action: Action, or the close, can be induced only by the proper presentation of the two preceding acts. This third act realizes the objective. It must be a knockout, regardless of the first two acts, or the play will be a flop.

Needless to say, the director (salesperson) who successfully presents the three-act drama of selling must possess and use imagination.

The imagination is the workshop of the mind in which is fashioned every idea, plan, and mental picture with which the salesperson creates desire in the mind of the prospective buyer.

Words alone will not sell. Words woven into combinations of thought that create desire *will* sell.

Some salespeople never do learn the difference between rapid-fire conversation that does not end soon enough, and carefully painted word-pictures that fire the imagination of the prospective buyer.

The sole object of neutralizing the mind of prospective buyers is, of course, to establish confidence. Unless confidence has been built in the mind of the prospect, no sale can be made.

THE TEN FACTORS
ON WHICH CONFIDENCE IS BUILT

By careful observation of thousands of salespeople, I discovered that ten major factors enter into the development of confidence. They are:

1. Follow the habit of rendering more service and better service than you are paid to render.

2. Enter into no transaction that does not benefit everyone whom it affects.

3. Make no statement that you do not believe to be true, no matter what temporary advantages a falsehood might seem to offer.

4. Have a sincere desire in your heart to be of the greatest possible service to the largest number of people.

5. Cultivate a wholesome admiration for people; like them better than you like money.

6. Do your best to live your own philosophy of business. Actions speak louder than words.

7. Accept no favors, large or small, without giving favors in return.

8. Ask for nothing of any person unless you believe you have a right to what you ask for.

9. Enter into no arguments with any person over trivial or nonessential details.

10. Spread the sunshine of good cheer wherever and whenever you can.

A MASTER CAN SELL ANYTHING

A master salesperson can sell a person anything that person needs, if the purchaser has confidence in the salesperson.

A master salesperson can also sell a person many things that person does not need, but a master salesperson does not do that. Remember, to be a master salesperson you must play the double role of buyer and seller. Therefore, you must not try to sell any person anything that you yourself would not buy if you were actually in the position of the prospective buyer.

Every successful business must have the confidence of its patrons. The salesperson is the intermediary through which this confidence is acquired—or lost. The master salesperson knows the importance of acquiring and holding the confidence of the buyers, so the master salesperson bargains with them as if he or she were the owner of the business.

High-pressure methods, exaggerated statements of fact, willful misrepresentation, and innuendo, destroy confidence.

If you are a salesperson who knows how to build the bridge of confidence to prospective purchasers, you may write your own ticket.

Some years ago, when almost everyone wore a hat, I knew a master salesperson who ran a chain of men's hat stores in Chicago. This store gave the guarantee that if the customer found his purchase unsatisfactory, he could bring back the hat, or any part of it, to the store and receive a brand new one in its place with no questions asked.

I was informed by the owner of the store that one man had been coming back twice a year, for more than seven years, and exchanging his old hat for a new one.

"And you permit him to get away with that?"

"Get away with it?" the store owner replied, "Why, man alive! If I had a hundred men doing the same thing, I could retire from business with all the money I need, inside of five years. Never a day passes that we do not trace sales to the talking done by this man. He is literally a walking and a talking advertisement for us."

That statement threw an entirely different light on the subject. I saw that this hat-store owner had built an enormous business on an unusual policy which developed confidence.

There are two major occasions which cause people to talk about a business: when they think they have been cheated, and when they have received fairer treatment than expected.

All people are like this. They are impressed by the law of contrast. Anything unusual or unexpected, whether it impresses favorably or unfavorably, makes a lasting impression.

THE ART OF CLOSING A SALE

The closing of a sale is said to be the most difficult part of the entire transaction. That is not true, however, if the groundwork has been properly laid. As a matter of fact, the climax of a sale is a mere detail if a sale has been properly made.

In almost every instance when a sale is hard to close, the difficulty may be found in some part of the transaction that led up to the close. If you are a master salesperson, you have carefully prepared your way to the close, step by step, through proper attention to the following details:

1. You have taken care to neutralize the mind of your prospect to make it receptive to your sales presentation.

2. You have made the mind of your prospect favorable by establishing confidence.

3. You have qualified the prospect's mind accurately to make sure that you are dealing with a prospect and not a mere "suspect."

4. Above all you have planted in the prospect's mind the most logical motive for buying.

5. You have tested the prospect, during your sales presentation, and have made sure he or she followed your presentation with interest. You do this by closely watching the prospect's facial expression and paying attention to his or her statements indicating a desire for the object of the sale.

6. Last, but by no means least, you have made the sale in your own mind before trying to close it. You know this by the "feel" of your prospect's mind. You cannot become a master salesperson without developing the ability to tune in on the prospect's mind. This ability, more than anything else, is the distinguishing feature of a master salesperson.

Having taken these steps satisfactorily, the salesperson is now ready to close the sale. There are thousands of salespeople who can arouse interest, which is the first step in the actual process of selling. And there are thousands who can create a desire for their goods or services, the second step. But at the third step they fall down because they lack the ability to close. Remember, if the advice in this book has been properly learned, the close comes easily and is nothing but a mere detail.

SUGGESTIONS FOR CLOSING A SALE

The following suggestions will be helpful, even to the seasoned salesperson, in developing mastery in closing:

I. Do not permit your prospect to lead you away from your sales plan by arguing over nonessentials or extraneous subjects. If your prospect insists upon breaking in, and tries to direct the conversation to build up an excuse for not buying, let it happen until the buyer has exhausted the tactic. Then tactfully switch back to your own trend of thought the moment your buyer hesitates. Go right along and develop your own thoughts to the climax. This is absolutely essential. Either the salesperson or the prospect dominates. It makes a great difference to the salesperson which one does the dominating.

2. Anticipate the negative questions and any objections that you feel
    exist in your prospect's mind. Beat the buyer to the punch. Ask
    and answer these questions yourself. But never bring up negative
    questions unless you are sure that your prospect has them in mind.
    In selling it pays to "let sleeping dogs lie."

3. Always assume that your prospect is going to buy, no matter what
    he or she says or does to indicate the contrary. Let the buyer know
    by your every word and every movement that you expect him or her
    to buy. If you weaken on this point, you are beaten at the outset
    because your buyer may be shrewd enough to observe that you are
    not sure of yourself. If your sales prospect suspects you are unsure,
    it will be used as an excuse to give you a negative answer when you
    try to close. The master salesperson never waivers for a moment. Be
    on the lookout for this sort of tactic and be prepared to negotiate
    successfully through opposition of this nature.

4. Assume the attitude that your buyer is right. The majority of
    mediocre salespeople make the mistake of trying to impress their
    prospect with their superior knowledge. This is usually poor sales-
    manship. Any suggestion that you make, by direct statement or by
    innuendo, that you are smarter than your buyer will antagonize the
    buyer, even though he or she may not show antagonism openly.
    Acting like a know-it-all has cost more than one salesperson the
    opportunity of making a sale.

5. When naming the amount of the purchase, set the figure high. It is
    better to come down if you find that necessary than it is to set the
    amount too low and then find yourself with no margin on which
    to trade when closing time comes. Even if the figure you name is
    out of the prospect's financial range, your assumption of his or
    her ability to buy at the larger amount will not offend your buyer.
    If, however, you make the mistake of underestimating your buyer's
    financial ability, you may offend. It has happened many times.

6. Use the question method to encourage your prospect to give you information about the points upon which you intend to build your sales presentation. Then refer to those points as the buyer's own ideas. This is among the most effective of sales tactics, since the buyer will naturally uphold any statement that he or she has made (or thinks they have made).

7. If your prospect wants to consult a banker, lawyer, spouse, or some valued adviser, congratulate the buyer on good judgment and caution. But you must then tactfully begin to plant the idea that while bankers may know the money-lending business, lawyers may understand the technicalities of the law, and wives or husbands or friends may be well-informed and loyal, the fact still remains that no one of them is apt to know as much about the goods or services you are offering as you yourself know. You have all the facts, while others don't have the time or sufficient interest to get the inside information. You might also subtly plant the thought in the prospect's mind that he or she knows their own mind and their own business better than any other person.

8. Avoid permitting your prospect to think the matter over unless there is a very logical reason for the delay. If the matter needs thinking over, help your buyer do the necessary thinking right then and there. Remember, an ounce of persistence at this point is worth a ton of cure afterward. The truth is that most sales that are lost could have been saved had the salesperson been persistent for a few minutes longer.

THE RIGHT MOMENT TO CLOSE

Much has been said about closing sales at the right psychological moment, but experience has proved that the majority of salespeople do not know what that psychological moment is. The psychological moment is the time when the salesperson feels that the prospect is ready to close. There is such a moment in every sale.

One of the major differences between a master salesperson and a mediocre salesperson is the master salesperson's ability to sense what is in the prospect's mind, aside from what the buyer has expressed in actual words.

When you sense the psychological moment for closing, name the amount involved in the purchase and proceed to close the transaction right then. A delay of a few minutes, or even a few seconds, may give the prospect a chance to change his or her mind.

If you find, when you try to close your sale, that you have misjudged the psychological moment, go back over your sales presentation again, bringing in new closing arguments that you have saved for just such an emergency. You will also need to work up a collection of emergency arguments if you are to succeed to the category of master of sales.

If you are a true master salesperson you never show all of your cards unless you are forced to. Even then, you don't show all of them at once. Always hold some back, just in case you have to make a secondary sales presentation to get the order.

The psychological moment for closing is something the salesperson usually has to sense, although there are times when that moment is obvious from the statements of the prospect or from body language and facial expression. The salesperson whose mind is negative, or who is lacking in self-confidence, often misses the feel of the psychological moment for closing, because the salesperson mistakes their own state of mind for that of their prospect.

On the other hand, this principle can also be made to work to your advantage. If a salesperson can transmit a negative thought to a prospective buyer (which everyone has seen happen), then a salesperson can also transmit a positive thought. And that is the real reason that you should always assume an attitude both in thought and manner that a sale will be consummated.

If the prospective buyer senses your eagerness to close a sale hurriedly, it is generally fatal because eagerness to close is always accompanied by lack of confidence on the part of the salesperson. Your eagerness (and your lack of confidence) are transmitted by words, facial expression, and the general impression you give off.

If the prospect gets the impression that the salesperson is eager to make a sale because that salesperson needs the money, the chances of making the sale are usually spoiled. The salesperson who has an air of prosperity in his or her personal appearance and tone of voice is usually a successful closer. The reason is obvious.

A master salesperson seldom asks the prospect if they are ready to close. If you are a master at sales, at the right psychological moment you will simply make out the order, conducting yourself as if the question of the sale were already settled. Asking the prospect if he or she is ready to close is the equivalent of expressing doubt that they are. But making out the order and handing it to the prospective buyer leaves no doubt about the salesperson's state of mind on the subject. The buyer usually reacts positively to such a suggestion—if the sales presentation has been properly made and the desire to buy has been planted in the prospect's mind.

Remember that the first place for you to close a sale is in your own mind. The whole world stands aside and makes room for you if you know exactly what you want and you have made up your mind to have just that. The salesperson who shows the slightest sign of hesitancy or doubt when the closing time comes, may as well not ask for the order.

I once trained a sales army of 3,000 men and women for a Chicago firm. Efficiency had to be the watchword, so before any salesperson was given a permanent job, they had to make a sale to at least one out of the first five prospective buyers called upon. On more than a few occasions salespeople called on those five prospects as many as a dozen times before a sale was consummated.

In the group of 3,000 salespeople, only 128 failed to qualify for permanent positions because they could not make a sale to the first five prospects. We taught these salespeople that "no" seldom need be taken seriously.

To make sure that our salespeople learned confidence, we set up our own "dummy" offices. In cases where we felt sure that all a new salesperson needed was a little more confidence, we included the name of one of these dummy companies in the salesperson's first five contacts. The dummy-company managers were instructed to give the salesperson a hard battle, but to let him or her win by making a sale. These sales went through, the commissions were paid on them, and the effect was astounding—especially in the cases of salespeople who had never tried to sell before.

We usually had the salesperson call on the dummy buyer last, after the four legitimate prospects had been called on. We found that after making the sale to the dummy, the effect was so encouraging that very often we could then send the salesperson back over the list of the four prospects and most of them would be sold on the second try.

It was obvious to me that the salesperson's state of mind has more to do with determining whether a sale is made than does the state of mind of the prospective buyer.

SEE YOURSELF AS YOU REALLY ARE

[This final section and questionnaire is excerpted from **Think and Grow Rich: The 21st-Century Edition.***]*

Your business in life is to achieve success. All success begins in the form of thought impulses.

You control your own mind; you have the power to feed it whatever thought impulses you choose. With this goes the responsibility of using your mind constructively. You are master of your own earthly destiny, just as surely as you have the power to control your own thoughts. You may influence, direct, and eventually control your own environment, making your life what you want it to be.

The following list of questions is designed to help you see yourself as you really are. You should read through the list now, then set aside a day when you can give adequate time to go through the list again and thoroughly answer each question. When you do this, I advise that you read the questions and state your answers aloud so you can hear your own voice. This will make it easier for you to be truthful with yourself.

SELF-ANALYSIS QUESTIONS

Do you complain often of "feeling bad," and if so, what is the cause?

Do you find fault with other people at the slightest provocation?

Do you frequently make mistakes in your work, and if so, why?

Are you sarcastic and offensive in your conversation?

Do you ever deliberately avoid associating with anyone, and if so, why?

Do you suffer frequently with indigestion? If so, do you know the cause?

Does life seem futile and the future hopeless to you?

Do you like your occupation? If not, why not?

Do you often feel self-pity, and if so, why?

Are you envious of those who excel you?

To which do you devote the most time—thinking of success or of failure?

Are you gaining or losing self-confidence as you grow older?

Do you learn something of value from all mistakes?

Are you permitting some relative or acquaintance to worry you? If so, why?

Are you sometimes excited about life, and at other times in the depths of despondency?

Who has the most inspiring influence upon you, and for what reason?

Do you tolerate negative or discouraging influences that you could avoid?

Are you careless of your personal appearance? If so, when and why?

Have you learned how to ignore your troubles by being too busy to be annoyed by them?

Would you call yourself a "spineless weakling" if you permitted others to do your thinking for you?

How many preventable disturbances annoy you, and why do you tolerate them?

Do you resort to alcohol, drugs, cigarettes, or other compulsions to "quiet your nerves"? If so, why do you not try willpower instead?

Does anyone "nag" you, and if so, for what reason?

Do you have a definite major purpose, and if so, what is it and what plan do you have for achieving it?

Do you suffer from any of the six basic fears? If so, which ones?

Have you developed a method to shield yourself against the negative influence of others?

Do you use autosuggestion to make your mind positive?

Which do you value most, your material possessions or your privilege of controlling your own thoughts?

Are you easily influenced by others, against your own judgment?

Has today added anything of value to your stock of knowledge or state of mind?

Do you face squarely the circumstances that make you unhappy, or do you sidestep the responsibility?

Do you analyze all mistakes and failures and try to profit by them, or do you take the attitude that this is not your duty?

Can you name three of your most damaging weaknesses? What are you doing to correct them?

Do you encourage other people to bring their worries to you for sympathy?

Do you choose, from your daily experiences, lessons or influences that aid in your personal advancement?

Does your presence have a negative influence on other people as a rule?

What habits of other people annoy you most?

Do you form your own opinions, or do you permit yourself to be influenced by other people?

Have you learned how to create a mental state of mind with which you can shield yourself against all discouraging influences?

Does your occupation inspire you with faith and hope?

Are you conscious of possessing spiritual forces of sufficient power to enable you to keep your mind free from all forms of fear?

Does your religion help to keep your mind positive?

Do you feel it your duty to share other people's worries? If so, why?

If you believe that "birds of a feather flock together," what have you learned about yourself by studying the friends whom you attract?

What connection, if any, do you see between the people with whom you associate most closely and any unhappiness you may experience?

Could it be possible that some person whom you consider to be a friend is, in reality, your worst enemy because of his or her negative influence on your mind?

By what rules do you judge who is helpful and who is damaging to you?

Are your intimate associates mentally superior or inferior to you?

How much time out of every twenty-four hours do you devote to:

- your occupation
- sleep
- play and relaxation
- acquiring useful knowledge
- plain wasted time

Who among your acquaintances:

- encourages you most
- cautions you most
- discourages you most

What is your greatest worry? Why do you tolerate it?

When others offer you free, unsolicited advice do you accept it without question or do you analyze their motive?

What, above all else, do you most desire? Do you intend to acquire it? Are you willing to subordinate all other desires for this one?

How much time daily do you devote to acquiring it?

Do you change your mind often? If so, why?

Do you usually finish everything you begin?

Are you easily impressed by other people's business or professional titles, college degrees, or wealth?

Are you easily influenced by what other people think or say about you?

Do you cater to people because of their social or financial status?

Whom do you believe to be the greatest person living? In what respect is this person superior to yourself?

How much time have you devoted to studying and answering these questions? At least one day is necessary for the analysis and the answering of the entire list.

If you have answered all these questions truthfully, you know more about yourself than the majority of people. Study the questions carefully, come back to them once each week for several months, and be astounded at the amount of additional knowledge of great value to yourself you will have gained by the simple method of answering the questions truthfully. If you are not certain about the answers to some of the questions, seek the counsel of those who know you well, especially those who have no motive in flattering you, and see yourself through their eyes. The experience will be astonishing.

THE ONE THING
OVER WHICH YOU HAVE ABSOLUTE CONTROL . . .

You have absolute control over only one thing, and that is your thoughts. This ability to control your thoughts is the sole means by which you may control your own destiny. If you fail to control your own mind, you may be sure you will control nothing else.

You were given your willpower for this purpose.

Highroads Media, Inc. is the publisher of more books and audiobooks by Napoleon Hill than any other publisher in the world. Other titles available:

REVISED & UPDATED

Think and Grow Rich: The 21st-Century Edition (hardcover)

Law of Success: The 21st-Century Edition

LEATHER-BOUND, GILT-EDGED COLLECTOR'S EDITIONS

Think and Grow Rich (single volume)

Law of Success (available in four volumes)

AUDIOBOOKS AVAILABLE ON CD

Selling You! (abridged audiobook)

Selling You! (unabridged audiobook)

Think and Grow Rich (unabridged and abridged audiobook editions)

Think and Grow Rich: Instant Motivator (original audiobook)

Law of Success (four-volume unabridged audiobook set)

Your Right to Be Rich (unabridged audiobook)

Napoleon Hill's Keys to Success (unabridged and abridged audiobooks)

Believe and Achieve (abridged audiobook)

The Richest Man in Babylon & The Magic Story (original audiobook)

A Lifetime of Riches: The Biography of Napoleon Hill
(abridged audiobook)

For more information about Napoleon Hill books and audiobooks, contact:
Highroads Media, Inc., 6 Commerce Way, Arden, NC 28704
telephone: (323) 822-2676
fax: (323) 822-2686
email: highroadsmedia@sbcglobal.net

visit us at our website: www.highroadsmedia.com